AW WITH WORDS

Young Writers' 16th Annual Poetry Competition

It is feeling and force of imagination that make us eloquent.

How can I not dream while writing? The blank page gives a right to dream.

Verses From
East & West Sussex

Edited by Mark Richardson

 Young**Writers**

First published in Great Britain in 2007 by:
Young Writers
Remus House
Coltsfoot Drive
Peterborough
PE2 9JX
Telephone: 01733 890066
Website: www.youngwriters.co.uk

SB ISBN 978-1 84431 136 1

Foreword

This year, the Young Writers' *Away With Words* competition proudly presents a showcase of the best poetic talent selected from thousands of up-and-coming writers nationwide.

Young Writers was established in 1991 to promote the reading and writing of poetry within schools and to the young of today. Our books nurture and inspire confidence in the ability of young writers and provide a snapshot of poems written in schools and at home by budding poets of the future.

The thought, effort, imagination and hard work put into each poem impressed us all and the task of selecting poems was a difficult but nevertheless enjoyable experience.

We hope you are as pleased as we are with the final selection and that you and your family continue to be entertained with *Away With Words Verses From East & West Sussex* for many years to come.

Contents

Filsham Valley School, St Leonards-on-Sea

Andrew Hall (13)	18
Bonizwe McFadden (12)	19
Yunus Tumi (14)	19
Kirstie Southcott (15)	20
Saif Ali (15)	21
Chris Adams (14)	22
Jamie Garry (14)	22
Chloe King (13)	23
Jamie Neal (15)	23
Tulasizwe McFadden (15)	24
Danielle Smith (15)	25
Kristina Terry (14)	26
Kelly Fairall (13)	27
Hannah Shone (13)	27
Emma Prentice (16)	28
Shaun Barkworth (15)	29
Elizabeth Hopkins (14)	30
Jess Jupe (14)	31
Tom Winch (14)	32
Emily Robinson (13)	33
Matt Viney (13)	34
Alex Russell (14)	35
Michelle Pooley (16)	36
Vicki Morgan (15)	37
Kieren Reffell (15)	38
Kirsty Bone (14)	39
Leanne Creasey (15)	40
Sarah Hazelton (13)	41
Ben Wood (15)	42
Ami Freed (13)	42
Rebecca Benge (15)	43
Naomi Cruikshank (13)	44
Jemma Neaves (14)	45
Sophia Ripley (14)	46
Amy Stevens (12)	47
Megan Young (15)	48
Robyn Dean (13)	48
Chris Webb (15)	49
Binny Shrestha (16)	49

Sam Maloney (13)	70
Nicholas Beynon (13)	71
Jamie Dickson (13)	71
Raj Patel (12)	72
Zach de Vries (12)	72
Jonathan Hibbs (14)	73
Alex Kelly (14)	73
Jack Stuart (13)	74
Matthew Harrison (13)	74
Jack Salter (13)	75
Marcus Hoare (13)	76
Ben Harvey (13)	76
Lawrence Job (14)	77
Tom Setterfield (14)	77
Simon Tarbet (13)	78
James Fyles (14)	78
Sam Cleife (14)	79
Adam Keet (13)	79
Daniel Long (13)	80
Ian Ifield (13)	81
Dan Edmunds (14)	82
Thomas Chambers (12)	82
Thomas Barrett (14)	83
David Bennett (13)	83
James Wickett (12)	84
William Hayward (13)	84
George Foden (13)	85
James Bryer (12)	85
Jonty Lockyer (13)	86
Matthew Badcock (12)	87
Jamie Shiel (13)	87
Laurence Pengelly (12)	88
Chris Candy (12)	88
Jake Stoddart (12)	89
Sam Joyce (13)	89
Harvey Heasman (12)	90
Ryan Gangloff (12)	90
Josh Fox (12)	91

St Mary's Hall School, Brighton

Emily Williams (14)	91
Emma Burgess (13)	92
Ciara McGrath (13)	93
Freya-Rose Tanner (14)	93
Jasmine Kilpatrick (12)	94
Julia Hollis (14)	94
Holly Welsh (14)	95
Nina Sarfas (14)	95
Esme Sarfas (14)	96
Emily Pearce (14)	96
Romina Duplain (11)	97
Sophie Mitchell (12)	97
Zaynah Al-Shamkhani (11)	98
Sarah Russo (13)	98
Olivia Mason (12)	99
Ana Whittock (13)	99
Charlotte Patching (12)	100
Sophie Ebeling (13)	100
Lily Oakley (12)	101
Evie Pattenden (12)	102
Yzzy Lancaster (13)	103
Amy Martin (13)	104
Rosie Moss (12)	105
Stephanie Robb (13)	106
Angela Needham (14)	106

St Paul's Catholic College, Burgess Hill

Ben Byrne (12)	107
Mina Fidal (11)	107
Tom Ward (12)	108
Brontë McDonald (12)	108
Jasmine Guerrero (12)	109
Jessica Bennett (12)	109
Hannah Brown (13)	110
George Francis (11)	110
Lucy Hardy (12)	111
Isobel Cowan (11)	111
Rory Gillespie (12)	112
Ellie Wilding (12)	112
Rebecca Harvey (13)	113

The Poems

Uncle Mark

Uncle Mark is so lazy
He sits on the sofa all day long
Watching everyone work,
'Nasmiha, vacuum the floor,' he'd say.

Uncle Mark is an excellent commentator
He sits on the sofa all day long
Commenting on everything,
'Nasmiha, that blue dress doesn't suit you,' he'd say.

Uncle Mark is a coffee addict
He sits on the sofa all day long
While coffee cups pile around him,
'Nasmiha, bring me a cup of coffee,' he'd say.

Everyone was frustrated till one day came
When Uncle Mark grew so fat that he couldn't move again!
Now his comments have changed,
'Nasmiha, get me out of this chair,' he'd say instead!

Nasmiha Nasrudeen (11)

2027, Sedative City

The year is 2027,
and she woke up in Sedative City.
She awoke heavy, and rooted to the dull,
dreamless earth. She saw the people, watered-down,
sepia-coloured disbelievers, trudging through with blinkered
views, diluted passions and stone hearts; something
so empty dragging them down
so heavily.

She saw deadened,
wounded children trailing pension
schemes, and watched hollow, gaunt faces
pass her by in mirthless, merciless debts to sorrow.
She walked through Sedative City, through the ashes of forgotten
heroes, dust kicked in their eyes from the salt skips
lying scattered and abandoned, under street
lights left on in the middle of the day

midst dim radiation beams.
She walked through streets echoing the
same emptiness mirrored in their eyes, bearing
sunburnt lawns smothered in fag ends and blunted nerves.
She saw twilight in Sedative City through a haze
of exhaust pipe fumes and scorched concrete,
in a bitter-tasting whirlwind of student
politics turned woolly fascism.

Sedative City owned
the new generation, born to the brunt
of the mistakes of their proud elders, the men
who believed God was on their sides, who sought to view a
picture of tomorrow through a child's eyes, and
wept when they saw the same things,
the same wounds, the same old . . .
and yet they held their tongue.

Anna Conway Vickers (18)
Central Sussex College, Haywards Heath

My Birthday, But No Different

The noise starts, she sits up
Pulls the covers around her shoulders
She prepares, it starts with a bang
A yell that hurts too much
A cry, a cry that the girl in the bed can't help.

What to do, she wonders
But she already knows - nothing.
She'll weep as all silent years
But she wants to scream
So loud, grab help
But instead
She sits and listens
And waits.

Until the hurting's over
But even then she doesn't sleep
She never sleeps
Ever.

Chloe De Salis (16)
Felpham Community College, Bognor Regis

The Night Life

The moon shouts hello
As the sun pleads to stay
The stars jump forward
Then sadly the sun walks away

The river is sleeping
The sea wakes up
The light has gone
And darkness has risen

The buildings close their eyes
The clouds start crying
And the roads moan with dissatisfaction
When night-time begins.

Davy Portway (11)
Felpham Community College, Bognor Regis

Early Sun

Your tight red anger
Its rings looped around my brain
Please just stop tearing my words apart
And igniting them with your flames
Just stop shouting
Your words fracture my brain
I don't want tomorrow's early sun
Corrupted by our fury
Seeping slowly through the curtains
Awkward and ashamed
So just stop pacing up and down
Turn away your burning eyes
Forget our
Screaming
Shouting
Silence
Before our flickering love dies.

Lucy Collins (16)
Felpham Community College, Bognor Regis

The Moon

The white moon stares at the world below
He is surrounded by stars
Sleeping silently
The moon smiles at the world
And the world smiles back.

The white moon looks down and sees rivers
Rivers that run rapidly
He sees planets
Large planets that spin around slowly.

The white moon laughs at the jokes
The stars tell him
The people on Earth admire him
The moon winks at the world
As he closes his eyes to sleep.

Georgia Harley (12)
Felpham Community College, Bognor Regis

Nightfall Murder

In the dark of night the thunder crashes
The lightning strikes and the wind lashes
The little boys scrabble back to their tents
Intent on no sleep.

The wind whistles and tents shudder
As the gale creeps round every corner
Like a wolf running through a dark forest
The rain smacked heavily against the canvas.

Within minutes the boys were sound asleep
But they were not aware that racing through creaky shadows
Dark and mysterious, his shadow bounced up and down the trees
He was there, but his presence was unknown . . .

As the ash on the campfire glowed a blood-red
None knew in the morning one of them would be dead
His axe gleaming in the moonlight
An evil shriek ran through his eyes
A single slash through the canvas
Left the silence unbroken
He raised his axe, his red eyes gleaming
No one would be screaming, he raised his axe.

With a single slash the corpse lay lifeless
But no one knew, apart from the shadow from Shadows Creek.

He fled through the forest in and out of the swaying trees
He'd been and gone, who would be next . . . ?

Anna Judd (12)
Felpham Community College, Bognor Regis

Snow

At night when no light shone
The falling of snow had just begun
Each one of them hit a roof or ground
Without even making a tiny sound
They lay there until it was a thick layer of snow
And they were so quiet, not a person could know

As morning came, children screamed with glee
And danced around so happily
They would wrap up warm and run to their gardens
And stamp around as the wet snow hardens
From the sky, snow kept falling
But it would be gone by tomorrow morning.

Rebecca Knowles (12)
Felpham Community College, Bognor Regis

The Joyful Stereo

The stereo stands silent
Its button eyes staring outwards blindly
Its mouth clamped tightly shut
Suddenly it springs to life with one flick of a switch
It starts to sing loudly and joyfully
Its eyes light up and shine with happiness
Its mouth opens wide with increasing volume
The stereo has come alive
To bring fun, music and pleasure
To all those surrounding it.

Aimee Robinson (12)
Felpham Community College, Bognor Regis

My Ice

I've got ice and it has bits of mud
It has bubbles too, lots of them just frozen
The colour of it is murky, browny-white
It came from the snow we had two days ago.

My ice came down from the sky
It got there from the clouds
From rain it turned to a puddle
Then went back up because of the sun.

When it was there it got dramatically cold
So it froze and turned to snow
Then when it was ready it jumped off the cloud
The same cloud that gave him the confidence to do it.

It fell and eventually hit the floor
And got picked up
It couldn't believe it, then with a thrust it got launched
Splat, what was that?

Matthew Yates (12)
Felpham Community College, Bognor Regis

Shoes!

I buy a pair of shoes and then I need another
A different shape, a different size, a different colour.
Red, yellow, green and blue
Different coloured dolly shoes.
Sometimes I have to wait in a massive queue
Just to buy a new pair of shoes.
Sometimes I get a brilliant deal
On a pair of hot, pink, high-heels
Shoes, shoes, I buy at the mall
Shoes, shoes, I love them all!

Luisa Embleton (11)
Felpham Community College, Bognor Regis

Little Red Riding Hood

Little Red Riding Hood
With her silky red hood
Merrily skipping along the path
Maybe her gran is having a bath?
A basket of goodies in her hand
With some pretty shells she found in the sand.

While she skips to her gran's
The Big Bad Wolf has some deceiving plans
As he opens the pine door
The little old lady hits the floor
He boots her into the wardrobe
Then he puts on her night-time robe.

Little Red Riding Hood knocks on the door
Now the wolf is the one who hits the floor
She goes inside and goes to the bed
But she gets a shock to see an irregular gran in the bed
Suddenly the wardrobe slammed wide
Scared the wolf stepped aside.

The gran karate-kicked him out the door
But the Big Bad Wolf hardly hit the floor
They shut the door
And the goodies they adored!

Jenny Skirrow (11)
Felpham Community College, Bognor Regis

Socks

Socks are fuzzy
Socks are cool
Stripy socks
I wear to school
Spotty, chequered, fluffy too
Red, pink, yellow blue
Long, short, wild and crazy
Ankle length even lazy.

Lauren Goodhew (11)
Felpham Community College, Bognor Regis

Our Beach

On our estate we have two beaches
My favourite part of the picnic is our peaches.

We see the waves
Curl into caves.

When Mum is bathing under the sun
We have a game of football and have lots of fun.

On our beach, in the sea we saw a great swish
All of us thought it was a whale, but it turned out to be a fish.

Billy, my brother, fell over the stones
Sadly poor Billy broke three of his bones.

Suddenly he fell into an enormous hole
Shaped like a beautiful bowl.

Mum said it's time to go home
We all started to moan.

My sister, dad and me went wild
But little Billy grinned and smiled.

Billy wanted to see our dog Ben
He said, 'I'm never going to the beach again!'

Hannah Corrigan (12)
Felpham Community College, Bognor Regis

Make-Up

Me and my friends are having a sleepover
We laugh and laugh all night long
We talk about boys but mostly make-up
There are eight of us giggly lot
We put make-up on in a silly way
I wish this sleepover would never end.

Emma Hanson (12)
Felpham Community College, Bognor Regis

Mirage

The hot blazing sun shines, baking the Earth
In the scorched desert I
Scurry, searching for a cool puddle of shade
My scales shimmer and glisten
And my eyes dart around in circles
Looking at the vast empty landscape.

Suddenly, a dark shadow appears just a few miles east
I am already exhausted and my feet
Bear shrivelled shining cuts and suppurating red sores
But that shade is *calling* and it seems I have no other option

Just as I come close, the refuge slips away
And my heavenly image mixes and swirls like a kaleidoscope
My journey begins once again.

Alex Oliver (12)
Felpham Community College, Bognor Regis

All About Me!

The start of my life was sad, dark and lonely
No family, no friends, no happiness.

The life I live now
Is full of happiness, friends and family
No tears as long and loud as a waterfall
The colour of baby blue.

The future me
Is all happy and full of good deeds
Work is a burden but I am happy
For I have a nice life and friends and family
I have a happy life, I hope I don't lose it!

Charlotte Law (12)
Felpham Community College, Bognor Regis

Untitled

As the day comes to an end
The shops whisper goodbye to the people
Darkness descends upon the street
The people say goodbye to each other
Buildings spy as people leave the empty street
The lights flicker, *on, off, on, off*
Trees casting shadows upon the street
The wind howls through the town square
Stars twinkle as they stare upon the town
As the sun rises another day to look forward to
Another night over.

Alex Chinery (12)
Felpham Community College, Bognor Regis

Snow

A white blanket all over the street;
Is the sight I woke up in the morning to meet.

The stars wink at the phenomenal sight;
And the moon gazes down on this wondrous night.

The scarecrows turn white and the cows very pale;
And the world seems to spin at the pace of a snail.

As the sun comes up and into the sky;
I get out of bed and look out of the window
I can't take my eyes off the astounding sight
It is . . . *snow!*

Poppy Brooks (11)
Felpham Community College, Bognor Regis

The Moon And Sun

The white moon sleeps in the bright daylight
And as the evening comes, the moon can show its pride
And show the world how it can make people happy.

Meanwhile, the sun is awake and shining
To a different place of wonders
It shines like it is God and smiles at the people
Who are enjoying it as if there was no night.

But people start to forget them and think they are nothing
Like they have disappeared into thin air
But they are still shining brightly in different places
Not always in sight.

Matthew Wood (11)
Felpham Community College, Bognor Regis

The Wolf Hunt

Midnight
A howl
A rustle
The wolves rise.

The hunt is on
Nothing will go wrong
Blood will spill tonight.

Flesh munched
Bones crunched
Red liquid drips onto the dirty ground.

Asleep now
Rest in peace
A life is lost forever.

Luke Sherwood (11)
Felpham Community College, Bognor Regis

Grass

The blade of grass started its journey
At the deeper part of the earth
After it had grown, it thought-tracked about its life
He remembered when he was wriggled over by slippery worms
And how the mighty ants showed their strength.

Then he cried remembering
How he survived the harsh weather
With the heavy cold snow.

Then when he was thinking
He was snatched from the ground by a giant
And ended up at school!

Jack Smith (12)
Felpham Community College, Bognor Regis

The Mountain

Perilous if you slip, merciless, unforgiving
Yet joyful and exhilarating
When you reach your goal

Up and up you go
Heading straight for the top
Nothing can stop you now
You're a power-house.

Adrenaline flows through your veins
You're there at the peak
Standing on top of the world.

Peter Nicholls (12)
Felpham Community College, Bognor Regis

Bunnies

Bunnies are white and grey
Possibly black, it's hard to say
They scurry around looking for food
Their manners have become very rude.

They have big ears to hear so far
Like an elephant without the weight of a car.

They stride along as if they're the queen
Looking and checking for danger it would seem
They don't cast smiles, they're grumpy all day
Boy, I wouldn't want to get in their way.

Stefanie Peffer (12)
Felpham Community College, Bognor Regis

Diamonds

Dead bodies lay before me, stagnant scents filled the air
The outcome of the struggle, for jewels that kings did wear
The sorrow and the pity, of all those that were lost
Would settle upon our hearts, in malevolent, icy-cold frost.

The menacing eyes of greed had robbed the whole land clean
A past full of evil haunted and shunned the scene
My heart bled with sadness as I gazed down upon
The land that I once knew, which had gone so terribly wrong.

The hills once laced with diamonds, were now a bloody mess
Innocent souls of victims would now eternally rest
Oh the pity, oh the shame, there's nothing left but tears
And the deep, dark dangerous caverns are laced with nothing
but fears.

Josh Blackman (14)
Felpham Community College, Bognor Regis

I Was Killed Today . . .

I was killed today . . .
But I'm still living
Living on the outside
Not on the inside.

I won't go to Heaven
And I won't go to Hell
But the person I want so much to be here
I won't see for a lifetime.

I will always remember
My memory lives on
The rest of me doesn't
The me I once knew, is no more.

I was killed today . . .
But I'm still living
Won't go to Heaven, won't go to Hell
And my memory lives on.

Mel Price (14)
Felpham Community College, Bognor Regis

A Day As A Wardrobe

Yes I am a wardrobe
Getting shut and open
My heart getting broken
Not loved
My day is so boring
I hear myself snoring

I wish I was a human
I wish I could walk
I wish I could talk
Then they would treat me with respect
I am just another reject.

Megan Thompson (14)
Felpham Community College, Bognor Regis

The Day The Snow Fell

The snow fell all around
It floated and swirled and laid on the ground
The grass had turned from green to white
Now it was time for a snowball fight!

The clouds were grey
The air was cold
The cars were stuck in the icy snow
Pick up a snowball, start to throw.

All the children start to play
Up on the hillside, what a day
It turns colder and starts to snow
Wonder what will happen tomorrow?

Rachael Sutton (12)
Felpham Community College, Bognor Regis

Fun In The Snow

Me and my best friend Emma
Spent winter together
Having fun in the soft cold snow
Sparkling brightly
Shimmering slightly
Playing in the soft white snow!

Christmas Day
There we lay in front of the warm fireplace
Hot, warm and cosy
Drinking hot chocolate slowly
Wondering what we would do today?

Jenny Jim (12)
Felpham Community College, Bognor Regis

Untitled

The writer of this poem is cool and daring
He does not like sharing
He is cunning and sly
And likes to eat pie
Even though it goes straight to his thigh.

He is as strong as an ox
And does not live in a box
He's quicker than a flick
And can smash through a brick
He has cool spiky hair
And has a pet bear
And wants to be a billionaire.

He is, he is the one and only
He is unique, special, he is
Me!

Ryan Keen (12)
Felpham Community College, Bognor Regis

The Sea

The sea is a mix of blues and greens
The sun shimmers down on the shining sea
The grey rocks at the bottom of the sea get disturbed
The brown, white and grey pebbles upon the shore
Get skimmed into the sea
Sea creatures flap their fins and swish their tails
Swim through the water past the rocks
Past the green and brown seaweed
The waves are like a bubble bath
All foamy and white.

Bronte Welham (12)
Felpham Community College, Bognor Regis

A White Winter

The cold blistering snow comes to England
Free-falling billions and billions of feet
Finally on its long journey it reaches the Earth
Then it will cover millions of miles in a white blanket
Soon, all the kids will throw it around
After the day is over, it will start to melt
It will turn into ice, then water
Then England will wait for a long, long time
Until the next white winter.

Chris Dahl-Hansen (12)
Felpham Community College, Bognor Regis

Bye-Bye Highbury

Highbury is gone but still lives in my heart
Sometimes in games I think Highbury played the part.

Highbury was good, I'm gonna miss it a ton
But I'm also glad the new Emirates is done.

Some people were saying the new shirt was gonna be black
But I don't think so, I think red is coming back.

I hope Henry don't go, I hope he stays here with us
So in next season's match, I hope I see him getting off the bus.

Time to go from the old and go to the new
Some people will be crying and some will shout yahoo.

Today was the final countdown on the 7th May
I know deep down I will never forget this day.

Highbury has been there for 93 years
And I know many supporters will shed some tears.

I wish I was an Arsenal player, that would be so cool
On the pitch with the others and kicking that ball.

Andrew Hall (13)
Filsham Valley School, St Leonards-on-Sea

Equality

You can't always be right or wrong
You need a bit of both just to stay strong
Humiliation is part of you but victory plays a key factor too.

People naturally want to be selfish without honesty
We cannot stop it . . . not even you and me
But the power of a third soul that is to be, or not to be.

Equality is a very strange thing
It can be the reason to not want to be a human being
To be equal is a rare thing because most people want to keep
their own things.

When the time comes for the legacy we shall need a team
Of that shall help us to see that the path to the destiny
If we lose, one thing shall be in our pride . . .
Yes with you and me our spirit from two different souls
That you can see to one soul with the power of two human beings.

Bonizwe McFadden (12)
Filsham Valley School, St Leonards-on-Sea

Inner Beauty

I am strange but you're just plain weird
Your hair needs combing, you're growing a beard
You're always sweating, you always smell
I know about your third nipple but I won't tell.
We can't have a civil chat without me noticing
You keep on playing and fiddling with your rings.
Whenever you talk to me it's not a human matter
Yeah, but no, but y'know, like whatever.
Your right leg's long, but your left one's short
You can't walk upstairs without your foot getting caught.
You can't dance, you can't sing, you can't do anything
You think you're hard with your flashy fake bling.
You're a butt-ugly monster causing everyone stress
But that doesn't matter, to me you're the best.

Yunus Tumi (14)
Filsham Valley School, St Leonards-on-Sea

You Used To Be Mine!

A year ago you used to be mine
Slowly over time I have been losing my mind
Day by day
Night by night
I now have realised
That life has no fairy tale ending
So I can stop pretending and start living my life
You said *forever*
But now I wish you said we would be together never
I thought you were the one for me
Living my life so carefully
Pushing me out when I wanted in
Holding my hand and holding me tight
Making me feel special, day and night
You told me we were in love
That God had sent me from above
Broken hearts and torn up letters
I knew we would never be together forever
Just like a fallen feather
Certain lyrics remind me of you
Doing what you always do
Being yourself and distant
Pushing me out when I wanted in.

Kirstie Southcott (15)
Filsham Valley School, St Leonards-on-Sea

Witness To A Battlefield

Allah. God. One and the same.
English. Arabic. The meaning? A name.
Religion.
Like the breath on the wind, whispering.
Religion.
Like a sigh from the sky,
The breath of life in a world of strife.
Religion.

Now in this time, with the rich, red, liquid death seeping,
Seeping through their uniforms, all smart and laced with gold
And silver trimmings.
And yet, strangely, no one is weeping,
Though Death comes a-creeping.
Death.
Though he sneaks here and there,
Holding a scythe that cuts, no *glides* though the air,
But he causes no pain, though he snatches their souls.
In passing he leaves one gift to the dead,
The dying and the living, all the same.
At once both a curse and a blessing,
Both a promise and a threat.
As he passes, a look of peace alights on each face;
Like the look one achieves with the loss of one's fears and woes.
Why don't we all look this way?
Every day.

But tomorrow will be exactly the same.
The problem is the ego of the leaders,
Seeking to dominate, wanting global fame.

Saif Ali (15)
Filsham Valley School, St Leonards-on-Sea

Getting Up In The Morning

When I wake up
There's a million different images
Running through my head.

I feel so drowsy
They don't even add up
That's why I stay in bed.

Then in comes my mum
Screaming and shouting,
'Get out of bed you lazy bum!'

I say why?
What's the time
Then Mum replies,
'Get out of bed, it's nearly nine.'

So I rush out of bed
As fast as I can
Gather my stuff
And jump in the van.

Chris Adams (14)
Filsham Valley School, St Leonards-on-Sea

Through Homeless Eyes

As I wake up and the cars pass by
I look up at the sky and ask God, why?
I just sit on the streets as quiet as a mouse
Wondering what it would be like to live in a house.
I just need a bit of money to start off a new life
And get away from all the drugs and the knives
People look down on me as if I'm a piece of dirt
Not knowing how much inside it hurts
I sit there in the same clothes
Feeling cold with a runny nose
I hate my life, I wish I was dead
I feel like putting a bullet straight through my head.

Jamie Garry (14)
Filsham Valley School, St Leonards-on-Sea

Wishes!

Wishing to transform the past?
Except all the unpleasant mistakes creates it a little too hard
Gazing through one eye and seeing the gloomy sky
Feels like smacking yourself with a slimy pie
Wishing for a touch to come back to life?
You'll just be heartbroken and you'll get out the knife
Wish for a smile to place on top of your face
Then bend down and tie up your lace.

You find wishes by wishing which turn into wishes
But can turn into horrid hisses!
Wishing is great
Wishing is fun
Wishing is something you can do one by one.

See a wishing sparkling star and make your wish
You might even get that special golden fish
Wishing too tough?
Then I would bring it to an end
This is something you definitely can't mend.

Chloe King (13)
Filsham Valley School, St Leonards-on-Sea

Smiting A Demon

There he stood, the big red man
I need to smite him with a mind-blowing plan
The big, tall, red man was a fiery-hot demon.
Man I must be out of my head, I must be dreaming
He shot a fireball at me
It misses me by the width of a bee
Now taste my guitar power
Playing a few strings sent a shower of lightning in his direction
Mortal, you're going to miss me
He screamed as he was hit by lightning,
'Huh, kiss me!'

Jamie Neal (15)
Filsham Valley School, St Leonards-on-Sea

Life As A Wonder To Myself

Why do we talk about life as if it is such a misery?
And yet, I didn't see things that bitterly.
I saw life as bouncy, prosperous and joyful too.
But as I became older in life, these things just
Seemed to disappear out of the blue.

One has to wonder to themselves
What is the meaning of life?

To achieve the best qualification one can get?
To make sure you get the best job attainable
So you can support you and your loved ones?
So that the children carry the family generations on?

No.
I see those as goals; nothing more
Surely the meaning of life is far simpler than that.

A wise man once told me
One day, much too soon, the end will come.
To each of our precious brief lifetimes
Knowing this, live fearlessly;
Leave unchallenged not a single obstacle between yourself
And the realisation of your most joyous dreams.

Working at the best of your abilities
Is the best thing one could ever do
It's what the rest of the animal kingdom do, isn't it?

Tulasizwe McFadden (15)
Filsham Valley School, St Leonards-on-Sea

Isn't It Amazing?

Isn't it amazing how . . .
One word can create tangents of thought
The heart
A scientific label for the chamber of life
Vital for the human's circulatory system
The skeleton of our emotions
One beat of the powerful muscle
Penetrating a detrimental day
Or commanding insecure respect.

The key to your heart
Clasped tight in the palms
Of those who you let get to you
With one rotation of this key
An unlimited stream of emotions can be set free.

A human being's words and actions can destroy a life
A day can bring greed, lust or rancour
But what matters the most
Is what you make of each hour
A minute can be wasted, of worries and fear
But a second can be extended
If led by enthusiasm and imagination.

Can you invent a substance of peace?
A potion of love, sharing and glee
Can you dream?
Can a dream come true?
If you wish with honesty and trust
The power of mind can conquer all
The power of belief drives to success
Although the thoughts of one person can evolve into words
So make your last words immune to regret.

Danielle Smith (15)
Filsham Valley School, St Leonards-on-Sea

Stars

Words are meaningless
They mean nothing to me.

You say the words
And scribe them on the stars
But stars are just as meaningless
As the deepest of all sonnets
As the most beautiful lyrics.

Stars do not show love or fear
Nor do they show anguish or hate
They just glisten in a diamond sky
Of pure dark divine.

I have lost my faith in words
Just as I have lost you
I can no longer read the stars
And feel the way I used to.

On the coldest nights
When everything is still
I look to the stars
And all I see is you.

How can sweet love become bitter hate?
Why is the sky so blue?
I don't care anymore
All I ask is why did they take you?

So young and so pure
I can't cry anymore
They have taken my tears as well
How can I say goodbye?
When you have not yet said hello;
To the world to life
You were too young to go.

Without you here
Words are meaningless
They mean nothing to me.

Kristina Terry (14)
Filsham Valley School, St Leonards-on-Sea

I Never Really Knew You

I never really knew you
But from what I've heard
You loved to make a good joke.

I never really knew you
But I can remember
You always used to sit in your chair
My mum sits there now.

I never really knew you
But every year at about the same time
We aren't as cheerful as normal
We're all missing you.

I never really knew you
But I will always remember you
And never forget you.

Kelly Fairall (13)
Filsham Valley School, St Leonards-on-Sea

Metacognition

Metacognition is a very long word
It's often a word few have heard.

Its definition is philosophical
It means thinking about thinking, which is so cool.

Once I think about metacognition
My mind has a collision.

What does thinking about thinking *actually* mean?
I don't like to intervene.

But thinking about thinking gets me thinking
Thoughts are moving and thoughts are linking.

Your brain is made of thousands of thoughts
Whether dreams of chocolate or, what is art?

Metacognition, I'm giving you the news
Is a clever word everyone should use.

Hannah Shone (13)
Filsham Valley School, St Leonards-on-Sea

Umbrella Creatures

Umbrellas are pets, the wonderful joy
They come in all colours and sizes
Have names
But aren't girls or boys
Alas! What a disastrous crime to give an umbrella a gender
How absurd!
When a name is a part of personality
Not meaning masculinity
Or femininity
They should be just that:
Unisex
Prominent
Personal
Proud
Oh Umbrella
Stevie
Brenda
Wigol Gorfishden you too
Gallop, drift float
Gracefully, peacefully, full of harmony
Now fly my pretties, fly.

Emma Prentice (16)
Filsham Valley School, St Leonards-on-Sea

Sense Of Control

My partner sits tight in my hand
To sense the torture and pain
Tonight was planned
I lurked in the shadows
Watching the minutes pass away
He showed but could not sense my presence
We were alone, him and I.

I pointed to the cold metal
The look of surprise on his shocked face
The truth was now blowing in the wind
I wanted to do it
I wanted to hear the bang and hear the scream
I'm turning into something I'm not
Just like in my dream.

I've done it, I fell to the floor
The crimson laced the pavement
The virgin snow disturbed
And a sudden bloom of blood on his head
I knew right then, I killed him; dead.

Shaun Barkworth (15)
Filsham Valley School, St Leonards-on-Sea

Take A Chance

Life is short but also sweet
Happiness is a feeling you just can't beat.
This is the way I look at life
I try to get through all pain and strife.
So if one day it gets you down
Take one day to sulk and frown.
Because this is the way I look at life
I try to get through all pain and strife.
Some day you will sit down and say
Yes, I'm going to die some day.
But this is the way I look at life
I try to get through all pain and strife.
So this advice I give to you
Treasure special moments for they will be few.
This is the way I look at life
I try to get through all pain and strife.
Make the most of every chance
Love, laugh and last dance.
So this is the way I look at life
I try to get through all pain and strife.
When I die it can never be too soon
And the words out of my mouth will be, I'll see you soon.
This is the way I look at life
I try to get through all pain and strife.
I'll know I've lived a wonderful life
Because I survived the pain and strife.

Elizabeth Hopkins (14)
Filsham Valley School, St Leonards-on-Sea

My Poem For My Missed Auntie

My auntie Mad, dearest of all
Who lived her life to the full
Until the day she laid at rest
She was and still is the best
The only one true to my heart
Having a sing-along she played her part
She enjoyed a drink
Double vodka I think
She treated everyone so fair
All she did was love and care
I can see you now dancing in the hall
My auntie Mad I seem to call
I love her dearly
And miss her clearly
Till death do us part
I know it's a marriage but it comes from the heart
I love you so
I'll try and let you go
Until we meet again
My best auntie
And special friend
I love you.

Jess Jupe (14)
Filsham Valley School, St Leonards-on-Sea

New Skills

Pushing myself to all levels
The most intense training I've seen
But I know that working hard
Will let me live my dream.

Jogging, jogging, jogging
That's the way it always goes
Never stopping for a rest
I hate the way it flows.

But you can't complain to the coach
You've got nothing good to say
But the hard work will pay off
For the big match the next day.

The coach is always shouting,
'Do what you're told.'
Freezing in the English weather
Puffing, panting and cold.

Caked in mud, waterlogged pitch
As the clouds gather, it's still raining
But at the end of the day
I'm learning new skills
I love my footie training.

Tom Winch (14)
Filsham Valley School, St Leonards-on-Sea

I'm The One That No One Wants

I'm lying in this damp cold cage
It's a misty-black and the ceiling's a dirty beige
Water's dripping slowly from my eyes
As people in wellies walk on by
They don't take a second look at me
Why is it that this can be?
Is it the same reason my old owners beat me
Or is it because I can't control my wee?
In my old home there was no one there to let me out
So when they would finally get back, they'd scream and shout
Wait, what's that, there's a young girl looking at me
She's laughing and pointing at my scraggy tail going all waggly
I run to greet her
As the cage is unlocked by my keeper
I sprint to my safe snugly bed
Because I got scared when she went to pat my head
My keeper comes and gets me and whispers in my ear,
'We've found you a new home, so don't you fear.'
She passes my lead to the little girl's mummy
I've got an excited feeling in my tummy
Uh oh, I've done it, I've weed again
But now the little girl comes over and says to me.
'Whoops-a-daisy, it's on the paper so don't worry Ben.'

Emily Robinson (13)
Filsham Valley School, St Leonards-on-Sea

Debut

Today is the day
The day of my first game
My first game for England
I'm standing with England's best 11
Today is the day

The kick-off is now
Now is my chance
My chance to show what I've got
I'm running on the pitch with England's star players
The kick-off is now

I've got possession of the ball
The ball is at my foot
My foot crosses the ball into the box
Rooney headers, it hits the bar and comes back to me
I've got possession of the ball

I just scored a goal!
The goal that just put England ahead
Ahead of the opposition
I ran the whole pitch and lobbed the keeper
I just scored a goal!

The final whistle sounds
Sounds from the crowds increase
Increase our chances of winning the World Cup
All eyes are on me as
The final whistle sounds.

Matt Viney (13)
Filsham Valley School, St Leonards-on-Sea

Heatwave Spirit

Glaring into the rippling ocean
I wonder where it is?
My shadow marks the pin-point
Of its daring heated bliss.

Some days I sit there dreaming
Of the structure of this creature
I play a game of chess
I say, 'I'm gonna beat ya.'

No reply is given to me
No words spoken or whispered in my ear
Is this thing just a vision?
Is it really here?

I feel a cruel unearthly sensation
The atmosphere is like it's never been
Am I being touched or poked
Or am I being watched and seen?

I tell others about this worry
They do not understand
Under the covers I lay
With the numbers 666 . . .
Written on my hand.

Alex Russell (14)
Filsham Valley School, St Leonards-on-Sea

The Destroyer

I'm the thing that makes that sparkle in your eye
I'm the one that lightens up the whole sky
I'm the thing that no one dares to touch
People don't really think of me that much.

I'm the most dangerous weapon in the universe
And deep inside I hold an evil curse
I glare at you all at least once a day
I watch you cry and I watch you play.

I hear you sing, I hear you talk
I watch you stumble when you walk
I feed the trees and the plants
And I watch the daisies dance.

But one day it will all fade away
Then no one will watch you cry and play
And there won't be any dancing or fun
Because I'll destroy it, me the sun.

Michelle Pooley (16)
Filsham Valley School, St Leonards-on-Sea

'Astings

I would love to see chavs bowling down the street
As the pier falls down in the summer heat
I would love to see the bus on time
No more old women in the line
And kids with kids in their prime
'astings full of grime.

The distinct reek of bottle alley at its peak
Weather as always, quite bleak
Old women stuck to benches in the street
Dive-bombing seagulls ready to give you a treat.

Everyone grumbles, the skies are grey
There's nothing to do and nothing to make you stay
Now I've spoke, I've had my say
I'm off home now, hope I haven't ruined your day.

Vicki Morgan (15)
Filsham Valley School, St Leonards-on-Sea

Winter

Following its course from east to west
The winter drifts in amongst the best
The winter weather following all the time
The snowflakes falling to the ground like a feather
The sun's rays gleaming at each of his cold friends
The snow forming a haven for the children
The rain falls like a tennis ball from a roof
The rain washes the snow down the drain
The children see the rain as such a pain
The tornadoes come and destroy the trees
It sweeps up the farmer's wide supply of peas
It carries the dog and savours the fleas
The tidal wave comes and causes people to drown
By now everyone's smile has turned to a frown
The fog casually enters the land while we sleep
Without making a sound or even a peep
You wake up to the sound of cars honking their horns, *beep*
The sleet comes down like a bowling ball from a shelf
The sleet damages monuments through all the lands
Destroying lives from east to west.

Kieren Reffell (15)
Filsham Valley School, St Leonards-on-Sea#

You'll Never Die

I think to myself when I'm all alone
How will I die which will never be known
Until that day my body is lifeless
My family are distraught, their lives are a mess.

I'm dreading that moment when I reach the other side
I'll be looking back on my life with a glint in my eye
Knowing every day I lived it to the full with care
I loved my family I wouldn't dare to break their hearts in such

a cruel way

Without saying goodbye on that sorrowful day

All the memories will be kept up inside of me
Everything will leave except the smiles I'd seen
Life is short and so live it while you're alive
As long as you keep remembering you'll never die.

I'm proud of myself to get this far ahead
Forget all the bad and say this line instead
I've done a few things I'll regret, stolen, hurt and lied
Life is about forgiveness and hopefully I'll die with pride.

Kirsty Bone (14)
Filsham Valley School, St Leonards-on-Sea

Love Or Not

I can't stop loving you
This pain you're putting me through
I know you hurt the people that you love
Does that mean you love me?
Tell me because I want to know
I'm not waiting for an answer
I'm not waiting for you
You're getting too much now

You say not to make a scene
But I want to know
When I'm with you I can't help but smile
My love is never-ending for you
But you don't seem to return your love back
Why do I bother?
It might be because I love you
My friends say you aren't worth my tears
I didn't believe them, but I am starting to
I tell them they don't understand
But they do
I love you for you
Not who you think you should be
I know I can't make you love me but I can try

I'm tired of trying
I'm tired of lying
I may be smiling
But deep inside I'm dying.

Leanne Creasey (15)
Filsham Valley School, St Leonards-on-Sea

What Have I Done To Make You Feel This Way?

What have I done to you
To make you feel this way?
Your eyes full of anger and hatred
They are starting to well with tears
The tears look as if they are about to flood out
Flood out like fire
Fire is the way your heart is, fiery and burning you inside
You feel anger but I only see the fear
What have I done to make you feel this way?
I thought you would never hate me but I guess I'm wrong
I feel cold inside
You have drained me of my warmth
Just by your cold-hearted looks
Your blood must be boiling
Your temper rising
I would never do anything to hurt you
What have I done to make you feel this way?
I see your hands twitch
I see your teeth grind
I see the burning pain in your eyes
You start to walk towards me
Getting nearer to me
What have I done to make you feel this way?
You walk past me
Not even a glare towards my direction
Not even a word
She has been like this for days
What have I done to make her feel this way?

Sarah Hazelton (13)
Filsham Valley School, St Leonards-on-Sea

Untitled

I stand staring at the emptiness
The cold, untouched, double bed upon which we lay
Oh how I crave the sweet comfort of laying next to you
Holding you in my arms as we kiss
I miss the loving touch of your warm body against mine
I miss the way we'd talk to each other about random occurrences
in our days
I miss all the times we would cuddle up in the bed and the way
you'd huddle close to me
I miss waking up and seeing your beautiful face in front of me

And now that happiness has gone
I don't see you in the mornings
I just see the boring beige wall with the window in the corner of my eye
I miss you!
I miss you so much.

Ben Wood (15)
Filsham Valley School, St Leonards-on-Sea

The Fierce Lion

The fierce lion lay upon the ashen rock
His teeth as sharp as knives which cut into crimson flesh
His blade-like claws grip onto the lifeless creature tightly
His golden mane glistening in the dazzling sun's beams
His large glassy eyes shimmer with delight as he rips his prey
He stands bold and tall like a mountain
His attention focuses on me
He races in my direction
His gaze then turned to me stabbing me like daggers
He pounces almost touching the sky and lands on my body
His bite draws blood on my pale skin
But no pain was felt and no marks were left
I heard his roar but it wasn't as powerful as before
His teeth were no longer sharp and his claws no longer grasped me
As the pain fades I drift gently back to sleep.

Ami Freed (13)
Filsham Valley School, St Leonards-on-Sea

Sorry

Why did it happen?
I regret it so much
If I could turn back time
Then you would have been mine.

As the years went on
I wondered why
I stole your life
And left it behind.

Now I sit here realising
That life is too precious
To take into one's own hands
Your life would have been great
And full of surprises
But I was too cruel
And took it away blindly.

Rest in peace my little one
For I did not know you
Nor did I love you
But that is in the past.

I was too young; too stupid
To be the right mother for you
Forgive me, my little one
For I now . . . love you.

Rebecca Benge (15)
Filsham Valley School, St Leonards-on-Sea

Desperado

Raindrops fell when the heavens opened
My hopes, dreams and wishes drowned
I stood standing
Relying on the cold teardrops that fell from my misty eyes
Heartache and pain struck my body
Like the seas, white horses hit the unprotected cliffs
I had put down my shield of armour
And now I paid for betrayal and all my deceitful acts
I walked alone
A deafening silence filled the streets
I am unknown.

I walked the never-ending roads a nervous wreck
My head tilted towards the floor so no one could see my lying face
It would be easier to get blood from a stone than to get
                              my head straight
My walk is so slow it has no pace
I am an utter disgrace.

Unfortunate companions are now long-gone
If only it could be the same for me
The memories and experiences engraved in my mind
I shall never forget fury or find freedom
I cannot trust another soul or I am hypocritical
I will never be sure again or feel love
At least I have one certainty
These awful deeds shall be with me for all eternity!

Naomi Cruikshank (13)
Filsham Valley School, St Leonards-on-Sea

Little Angel

Stop the world for today's the day
Prevent the baby's cry, silence the talking and turn the TV off
For here comes her tiny coffin, 'bout two foot long.

You left us before we even got to know you
Yes, we've held you, but never heard you
Oh, what I'd give just for you to cry

At least you felt no pain; we've felt it for you
You left us the moment you were born
And now we sit in a big lonesome church

And just for a little white coffin
You've gone now, but what's the colour of your eyes?
Why did you go? For what purpose?

Someone once told me we all have our time
And when we are needed, He will take us as angels
So I believe that's where you are and why you went

You will always be my little angel
But the pain's still there and will never go
For even before knowing you, I love you, you're the apple of my eye

You see, we take these things for granted
And just assume it will be all right
But now we know, those things you love, get taken away and hurt you
So goodbye, my love, my little sister, my little angel.

Jemma Neaves (14)
Filsham Valley School, St Leonards-on-Sea

Murder On My Knife

I glare through iron bars
Trace my finger down cold rust
Sense the psychotic minds of murderers
Taste the pride and regret for their awful sins.

Thoughts pulsing through my mind
I don't belong here. I'm innocent!
I'm not like them
But they know the truth and secretly so do I.

The beast smiles and smirks with glee
The beast within me the one that ensnared me
A night of an innocent's execution
The only catch is I was the executioner.

I severed her flesh, I crushed her ribs
I slaughtered her organs, I ripped her arteries
Body pulsing, crimson regret
Another life just slipped through God's fingers.

But something so satisfying feels so guilt-ridden
It's too much. So I thieve the gun
Direct death firmly on my temple
Close my eyes, inhale for the last
Another life tossed aside by God's hands.

Sophia Ripley (14)
Filsham Valley School, St Leonards-on-Sea

Our Reason For Living

What is our purpose here?
Why do we live?
Who are we inside?
What motivates our life?
So many questions I ask myself each day
Why do I wonder, tell me - what do you say?
Am I in myself, one who disagrees?
Am I in myself, one who needs things for free?
Who am I? What is my purpose - I'd really like to know?
'Money,' I say to myself
That's why I'm here.
That's all we want - our everlasting supply
We are just mere visitors here
On this planet we call home.
'But no, it cannot be,' I hear you yell,
'We must be worth much more than that!'
What happened to love?
Where did it go?
What happened to the world of lust and desire?
Some say it's still here but I don't
In the world of today - in our modern day life -
We are but mortals with no time to show our feelings
No time to stop and think
Why is it we don't take the time to look at what we've got?
No mortal stops to look around and take the beauty in
No mortal goes to work each day and loves what they are doing
Every mortal travels to work and thinks, *Oh well, it's for the money.*
We look at our life and take it all for granted
We treat the animals and plants as if they don't exist
Our purpose on this Earth, it seems, is to ruin it completely.

Amy Stevens (12)
Filsham Valley School, St Leonards-on-Sea

Losing You

Stop all the people, all the cars
Prevent the laughs with the sadness of our loss
Silence the church bells with the drowning of our tears
Bring out the coffins so we can face our fears.

Let us remember the goodness of your heart
With us loving you just the way you are
You're going away is our loss
Rest in soft peace, my long love lost.

Losing you was the hardest part
Like someone took a knife
And drove it right through my heart
For I wait for that day when we will meet again.

Wherever your head may lay
Among our hearts is where you'll stay
I never knew you as well as I think
But to be truthful you're my missing link.

Megan Young (15)
Filsham Valley School, St Leonards-on-Sea

My Lifeline

I reach towards your bedroom door
You're paler than I remember, smaller
Dwarfed by the double bed, you raise your arms
They shake, held by rebelling muscles and weakening bone.
We embrace; your painted lips brush my cheek
My lifeline holds me tight, a single thread spanning through the years
You smile, ask the questions then we depart
I know you might not be here next time I come
My lifeline falters, a wheeze, a cry, I fall;
Red lips mark my cheek, memories mark my mind
My lifeline falters, a wheeze, a cry, I fall . . .

Robyn Dean (13)
Filsham Valley School, St Leonards-on-Sea

Trick Poem

The trick with writing a poem
Is to keep the rhythm flowing
Then the reader without knowing
Will forget you're not really a poet.

With more than two verses, oh wait, they're called stanzas
You'll attract men and women and even a few pandas!
From far and wide people will come
To read your poem, for enjoyment and fun.

So now you sit in your mansion, feeling all smug
Looking down and laughing at your million dollar rug
And you think to yourself, for a word that describes
How people have acted to your poem of lies
You think long and hard, until it starts to bug
Then eureka! You've got it, they acted like mugs.

Chris Webb (15)
Filsham Valley School, St Leonards-on-Sea

True Friends

True friends are ever together
Who are meant to support each other
In the journey of life as they gather
And are supposed to help, forever.

They are the one to make you smile
Walk with you to cover miles
Doesn't matter if they are longest as the Nile
But are still there to make you feel joy in piles.

They are the only one who hold your tear
Make you feel they are near
Always say you are my dear
Then tries to make you rid of fear.

Finally, I'm writing this poem
Just to let you know, *friend*
I'm always there . . .

Binny Shrestha (16)
Filsham Valley School, St Leonards-on-Sea

Guilty

Why can't anyone hear my song?
I've kept this inside me for so long
Locked deep down, where it can't be found
Blood pours down from my swollen eyes
I'm finally stripped clean of my disguise
And now I'm bare for all to see
To see the mess that's really me
I'm unwanted, forsaken and hated by all
In my life I seem so small
Insignificance superior, emotions inferior
Why can't I just disappear?
I'll melt into that of everything I fear
Forgive all of my sins, run from my strife
Hide, hide from reality, hiding from my life
Hypnotised by guilt and sacrifice
It's time for me to pay the price
Those I love strike me down upon my knees
Torture me, record my screams
Dampen all my wildest dreams
I feel so dead inside, lifeless
I have so many questions left unanswered
But who's there to answer them?
No one, silence, emptiness, all at fault
Cut all the feelings I try to contort
And spread for all to see
But I can't stop feeling
So guilty.

Jade Worboys (15)
Filsham Valley School, St Leonards-on-Sea

Clocking Off

I see way up high
Clinging to my wall;
Watching over you
Like a guardian angel.

Giving you advice
Is how I spend my day
Watching everybody
Come and go away.

Occasionally, when you are bored
You turn to look at me;
When my hands tell you 'time for break'
You leave the room gratefully.

You will always depend on me;
I am like your rock
When you want to know where to be
You check your trusty clock.

Kane Tugby (17)
Filsham Valley School, St Leonards-on-Sea

Secret

Climb through
The Amazon rainforest
Around great buttresses
Of mighty trees
And humble plants
That cling to the ground
Till you reach a secret
A hidden pool
Never seen by any human till now
And a beam of sunlight
Dapples dreamily
Through the emerald leaves
Until it falls
Green-gold
On the pure ice-cold waters
Of the animals' secret place
Let's keep it that way
Protect the rainforest.

Lydia O'Sullivan (12)
Herbert Shiner School, Petworth

Stone Statue

I cannot feel anything
My fingers are frozen
I cannot see anything behind me
My eyes, I cannot move
I cannot smell anything
My nose is immovable
I cannot hear anything
My ears are stone
I cannot taste anything
My tongue is a rock
I want to be awake, warm and free!

Oliver Palfrey (9)
Littlegreen School, Chichester

The Town

Under the darkness of the cold shivering sky, where stars
like little light bulbs glowed
The tiny shops were darkened by the bigger
and more ginormous shops' shadows
I heard the clock bang as it struck midnight
The high-pitched whistle of the wind could be heard
in the dark empty town
The taste of stale beer and cold chips filled my nostrils
The feel of the icy air as it raced past me, brought a chill
racing down my spine
The stench of bitter, sour beer splashing on the frozen pavement,
made my stomach turn inside out
Empty chip bags rustled along the floor as I passed
As the wind roared through the air, the branches drummed
on any buildings in their way
And the rain pitter-pattered on the rooftops.

Sean Butcher (12)
Midhurst Intermediate School, Midhurst

The Funfair

The wind whips and whistles
As it rips the leaves off the trees
Bits of rubbish scrape violently across the floor
The roundabout screeches quietly around.

The laughter and life cease to exist
And now the darkness and deafening silence settle in
The touch of frost spearing at my legs
Coldness becomes a searing pain.

The black dismal night wraps itself around me
Crushing your every movement into a standstill
Sight fading, taste-crumbling, ears blocking
A quiet laugh floats in the air as I fall to the hard ground.

Elliott Harding (13)
Midhurst Intermediate School, Midhurst

As Day Turns To Night And The Clock Strikes Twelve . . .

As I wander through the school of tonight
I wonder what it will be tomorrow?
Rattling windows, tell their tale
As inside me my mind goes stale
The silent whispers through my ears
The echoed footsteps through my spine
A discarded jumper like a pool of blood
Pages fluttering like a sea of birds
Next to the shadowy church the night school stands
The moonlight beaming into airless classrooms
The corridors bare, with the air blowing around my ankles
The smell of rotting carpet, the dripping of a tap
The taste of imprisonment, makes me want to break free
The long-gone laughter, shall never return.

Lisa Prudente (13)
Midhurst Intermediate School, Midhurst

Funfair

The stale smell of candyfloss floating in the air
A carousel blowing in the background
Ghostly sounds going down the slide
Moss growing on the side of a helter-skelter
The echo of children
Half-eaten food left lying around
Something moving out the corner of my eye
Like a fox scrounging around
Rain splashing down
Like a drum beating on my head
A clock bell strikes midnight.

Andrew Jolly (12)
Midhurst Intermediate School, Midhurst

Gothic Poetry

The mist thickened and there was a frost in the air
I could not see the local church, but I did not seem to care
I lost my footing ages ago and now I'm in too deep
The trees are winding round me and my skin now starts to creep
The owl is hooting early, the badger shuffles by
I wish I wasn't in here - I may even start to cry . . .
I lost my footing ages back and now I'm in the dark,
dense forest without a soul in sight
The mist has thickened densely and I'm in the dead of the night.

Willow Arran (12)
Midhurst Intermediate School, Midhurst

The Truth

When I'm on the beach staring at the sunset
And a seagull flies past I ask myself in the depth of my mind,
'How does he know where is he going?'

Going, going, don't leave, stay
What, who and where?

When I'm lying in my bed at night staring at the stars
All shining in my face then I ask myself in the back of my mind,
'How and when did they get there?'

How, when
Stars are the stars?
Why, how and who?

Is it true what a mirror sees
Or does he change his mind?
Does he break at the sight of ugliness
Or is it just a spell?
I ask myself in the depth of my mind
Does he have a face like ours hidden beneath the glass?
Hidden, hiding
Show your greatness to the world
Shine, shimmer and rise.

Storm Chiverton (12)
Midhurst Intermediate School, Midhurst

Descriptive Writing About Tesco

Under the dark shadowy sky
Where the shimmering moon shines down
Windows shatter in the empty deserted coldness
Whistling of the wind with frost scattered everywhere
Sky as dark as a blackboard
The rattling of trolleys sends a shiver down my spine
Silent but deadly sounds fill the area
Wind blowing under the door
Shelves clatter as they fall
Sudden streaks of silence yet I can hear clashes in the distance
The smell of rotten fish fills my nose
Bins begin blowing and so it continues.

Sarah Bottriell (13)
Midhurst Intermediate School, Midhurst

Church

The bitter coldness of the church
The still silence of the bells
The sweet smell of pine pews
Lay motionless in the gloom of darkness.

Confetti floats across the floor
Like litter in a rubbish tip
The colourless glass windows
Rattle and shake in the vicious winds.

In the still night air
Where the frost has breathed its raw breath
The odour of death hangs
Like an oppressive force.

As I stand and watch
In the murk that smothers me
There are no noises
There are no creaks
Only the penetrating sound of silence.

William Cotton (12)
Midhurst Intermediate School, Midhurst

Funfair

3am at a funfair
Wind rattles the rides
Still the hovering smell of onions and burgers fill my nose
Birds attacking the lifeless ground hunting for life.

Lights flicker
Grass crackles with the frost
The sky is bare only a few stars dare to show
Gates crash behind me.

The noise of the music still echoes through my mind
The merry-go-round jumps out
The animals wait for the moment to spring
Sending shivers down my spine.

The teapots screech as they rock from side to side
Sweet wrappers rustle like a crackling fire
The roller coasters hold a piercing scream
This is 3am at a funfair.

Charlotte Vincent (12)
Midhurst Intermediate School, Midhurst

Snow

G listening, glistening
L aying in the streets
I t's like a blanket
S ewn over the houses
T he trees are like candyfloss
E veryone's looking outside
N obody makes a sound
I t's here, winter's here
N ow the snow is falling
G listening, glistening.

Alexander Piggott (11)
Midhurst Intermediate School, Midhurst

Past A Far Land

Past a far land
A black mountain stands tall
Behind the black mountain
Shadowy trees form an inky wall.

The shadowy trees
Are the only things in sight
While a looming tower
Blocks the sun's light.

The tower soars
And disappears in the sky
While from the top window
Is heard a wailing cry.

The top window is high
Up crumbling stairs
Along black corridors
Dusty portraits stare.

The dark corridor leads
To a small cramped room
While outside the door
Lays a long-dead groom.

Inside the room sits the bride
On a rocking chair
She weeps and wails
And cries her despair.

Georgie Bicknell (12)
Midhurst Intermediate School, Midhurst

London Underground Station

The shadow of the moon creeps through the door
As the crumpled papers are whispering along the tracks
The shadows of rats scuttling along the wall
The smell of tobacco rising like smoke from a fire.

A flickering light is now dead
Chips squashed by the hustle of life
Stretching forever the pillar's shadow
The pillars are tree trunks holding the roof of life.

The ticking of the clock, signalling another hour of the continuous
cloudy life
The crisp new packs of crisps that stand in the hard running
vending machine
Looked old, lifeless and dead
The firm wind was rustling around the pillars like a lonely witch
hunting for company
But just falling deeper into the tragic afterlife.

Spreading like a disease, the crack on the wall
On the platform, where the people stood, the non-stop hustle
and bustle of life
Was gone and empty
The sound of the trains had vanished into thin air
Like ice into water and then deathly into air.

The smell of chip fat was so overpowering I could taste it
The Devil crept around me, it was yesterday's papers
The darkness was creeping around like a lost puppy
Whistling wind was whining desperately waiting for its undisturbed prey
Quiet, it's very, very quiet . . . too quiet.

Matthew Cella (12)
Midhurst Intermediate School, Midhurst

Remembrance Of The Soldiers

Men and women everywhere
Wear poppies on their person
For all those men
All those years ago
A minute for the dead . . .
But not forgotten
Shot down in red fields
Through gun, armour, sword and shields
This is a funeral
They fought for our country
The one in which we live
We learn, we earn
This is an annual funeral
But we don't wear black
We wear red to respect our dead
It's not much to pin a poppy on your shirt
When you think of all those men choking on dirt . . .
But it's a lot to fight for your country
So be grateful
That you are here
As we bow our heads in silence
That those warriors fought
Through blood, panic, pain and fear
Pray and give thanks for those men
With a clear conscience . . .
Thank you for your sacrifice, your bravery
We respect you in every way
Though you are long since past
You are still the men of today.

Katherine Vallender (13)
Midhurst Intermediate School, Midhurst

The Park At Night

The swings creak as the wind blows
Knocking them to and fro
The raindrops on the seats reflect the moonlight
Creating an icy glow.

Fish and chip papers create a carpet
Roughly laid on the ground
Like crooked floorboards
As you step, that creaking sound.

The slide coiled round a pole
Like a snake hunting
On the prowl looking for food
Slithering through the grass, crunching.

The climbing frame stands silently
Waiting to be used
The monkey hoops swing in the wind
Reminds me when you fall off, scarred and bruised.

The football pitches with a goal at each end
A dead pigeon caught in the net
The stench fills the air, almost knocking me out
Right until the end.

The pain I am feeling this sinister night
From a place that should be full of life
Silence echoes through my rattled mind
And as the tears roll, you don't know what you'll find.

Lauren Gilson (12)
Midhurst Intermediate School, Midhurst

Love

I thought that this was just made up
I never realised it was true
Until I felt the strangest feeling
So wonderful and full of hope
It didn't stretch to everyone
It stayed with just one person
It was great to feel this way
Though the truth does have it
I felt like this
On more than one occasion
For more than just one person
Though nowhere near as strong
It was great while they were here
I thought it could, I thought it would
Go on forever and ever.

But then they left
I was so scared
I thought this feeling would diminish
Just go away when they did
I wanted to keep this feeling
For longer than they stayed
I was so scared
In case it went
I thought it would just go away
Or maybe fade away
But to my surprise it didn't
To my surprise it stayed
And now I know
That's why they call it
Love.

Abbie Souter (12)
Midhurst Intermediate School, Midhurst

Why Me?

Darkness, a blinding darkness
Silence, a deafening silence
I'm so cold, there's a burning chill
My body is frozen
Frozen in motion
My screams are muffled
Muffled by the silence
My legs and arms are as pale as a ghost
My stomach is a bottomless pit
My throat is a desert - choking to be watered
My confidence; crushed
My world; destroyed
I try to get out
I try to fight
But I'm weak and tired
Why am I here?
Why me?
What did I do to deserve this?
What crime did I commit?
Imprisoned by a man
Not even worthy to be called a man
A coward
That makes girls like me suffer
For pleasure
It makes me sick
Please someone, find me
Please hurry for me
I'm running out of time
Please hurry.

Anna Goodman (13)
Midhurst Intermediate School, Midhurst

Black And White

When it's night
And I'm in bed
I wonder
When does the forest sleep?
When do the rivers rest?
When do the animals hibernate?
When does the hustling and bustling of the animal kingdom end?
The world rests
When it is black and white.

When is the world
Tucked up in bed?
I wonder
When is the world under glistening covers?
When does the world rest?
When does his mother whisper goodnight?
The world rests
When it is black and white.

The world rests
When his glistening blanket falls
When the colours make way for something new
When the world rests he is covered in cotton wool
And people he only sees in winter
The world is black and white.

The world rests
When the world is an old TV
When the world is black and white.

Scarlett Harris (11)
Midhurst Intermediate School, Midhurst

The Flying Pig

'How boring life is,' said a pig one day,
'Wouldn't it be great to just fly away?'
And just like that
He leapt off the mat
But landed snout first in the hay!

Hum, he thought, *this isn't right*
I must make changes for my next flight.
So he climbed up his sty
And set out to fly
But still didn't reach a desirable height.

'Ouch!' he cried as he fell to the floor,
'What should I do? I don't know anymore.'
Then came an idea . . .
But trembling with fear
He jumped off a cliff top by the seashore.

Bang, thud, splat, was the terrible sound
As poor old piggy crashed to the ground
And whilst he lay there
He caused a great scare
As people gathered from miles around.

The news spread fast, quick and loud
About the pig who is to be found
Flying so high
High in the sky
On his very own white fluffy cloud!

Tanya Wilson (11)
Midhurst Intermediate School, Midhurst

Mirror

Does a mirror lie upon the face that looks at it?
Does a mirror tell you the truth or does it hide ugliness?
Is a mirror amazing or something that makes someone cry?
Because nobody knows if a mirror has a mind of its own
Nobody knows what a mirror thinks about you
Nobody knows what a mirror holds.

Ffion Parry (12)
Midhurst Intermediate School, Midhurst

The Swing

Autumn leaves
A fiery shower
Deplete summer's shady bower
In a sea of red and gold
Russet, brown and greeny mould
And from the oak tree still hangs
Defying frost and winter pangs
A wooden swing
With strings of cord
My almighty flying lord
On which I sat
Through sulks and smiles
Which bore my weight
Through many trials
On this I sat
And flew so high
I think that even birds passed by
Defying laws of gravity
And it was only mine, for me.

Thea Challen (13)
Midhurst Intermediate School, Midhurst

War Memories

The sound of screaming is heard
When I close my eyes
A ringing through my head

A picture is built
When I close my eyes
People lying dead.

Shouts and cries
Yells and screams
Are filled up in my mind
But the question I am asking
Why isn't the world so kind?

Guns and explosions fill my body with fear
A tremble up my spine
But suddenly all goes silent
I know it's my time.

Libby Brewster (11)
Midhurst Intermediate School, Midhurst

Fire

First a spark
Then a flame
It lights the sky
It plays a game.

As black smoke rises
Creeps through the house
It claims its prizes
Invades their lungs.

Orange, white, yellow, red
The colours flicker, intensify
Killing people in their bed
But how can death be so beautiful?

Katy Ellyatt (11)
Midhurst Intermediate School, Midhurst

Footballer

He strides across the open field
Kicking and flicking the ball
His legs muscly and his arms strong
His shadow long and tall.

Running like an athlete
His eyes focused on the aim
The goal from a long distance
It's going to be a tiring game!

Hot flushes are coming on
His hair in his face
The crowd cheering him on
His kit in a disgrace.

Lauren Eves (11)
Midhurst Intermediate School, Midhurst

War For The World

Bang! Bang! Bang! went the guns
Most of them were killed for fun
Everyone else ran
Ran for their lives
Some were shot down
In front of my eyes.

See all the planes flying by
Some got blown up in the sky
Some might be your friends and family
Some might be a stranger from the army.

War is a terrible thing
People die and people flee
Also think of those who fought for us
Think of those who died for us.

Fergus Penfold (13)
St Andrew's CE High School for Boys, Worthing

Winter

Snow lightly falling from the sky
Sun poking out from behind a cloud
Like we have been in darkness for years
Snowmen spotted in gardens waiting for people to walk by.

Frozen lake of ice
It is really nice
To see the children play
All night and day
Having fun in wintertime
Around the beautiful pine trees.

Sam Jones (12)
St Andrew's CE High School for Boys, Worthing

Cats

I love cats they are the best
I think they are better than the rest
I love the way they are grey
When they go to the toilet or their litter tray
But they do get fleas but don't get nits.

When I sleep in my lovely bed
There is my cat above my head
She sits on the fence and miaows
Trying to make a midnight howl
When I wake up she wants food
Then she miaows being rude.

She is as black as the night sky
She miaows and cries, cries, cries
She isn't a fat cat
She's a lazy mat
I love my cat Izzy
I want another cat to live with me.

Max Watkinson (12)
St Andrew's CE High School for Boys, Worthing

Fish

Fishing has a way with words that say, hook line and sinker
The hook swings as smooth as a brainwave
The line dashes as fast as Wayne Rooney
The sinker sinks as fine as worms playing poker
And a fish caught faster than Speedy Gonzales.

Richard Taylor (12)
St Andrew's CE High School for Boys, Worthing

Running In The Woods

I am running through the woods
Leaves and branches are whipping past my face
My heart is pounding against my chest
Birds launch from trees as I dash past
Leaves crackle beneath my feet
Cool air rushes past my face
The sun bursts through gaps in the canopy of leaves
The trees all blur into one.

My breathing turns to a rapid gasp
My legs feel like lead as I try to go
Faster, faster and faster
Sweat is dripping down my face
I carry on relentless of the pain in my side
My heart is hammering inside me
My face is as hot as the sun
And is as red as blood.

My legs slow and I drop to the ground
My lungs struggle to suck in enough air
I lay there for minutes on end
I get up still panting and look back
All I can see is row upon row of trees
I begin to walk home across the green rolling hills of the South Downs
The sound of birdsong in my ears.

Sam Maloney (13)
St Andrew's CE High School for Boys, Worthing

Young Writers - Away With Words Verses From East & West Sussex

Love

Girl and boy, love in the middle
Love is in the air
Wearing PJs as soft as clouds
Moving lovingly
Gazing at each other in a bed
Going to get married
On a summer's day
Then they're together
Love, love, love.

Nicholas Beynon (13)
St Andrew's CE High School for Boys, Worthing

Fear

No one sees *me*
No one understands *me*
Blind, blind to all *colours*
Draped in robes of *darkness*
Blackness
Swamped in the fear of all things great and *small*
Always cover my *tracks*
Watching
Crying
Screaming
Help
Help
Help me please . . .
Silence
Nobody comes, *no one*
Darkness
Fear
Hell . . .

Jamie Dickson (13)
St Andrew's CE High School for Boys, Worthing

Hatred

On your shoulder or in Hell
He knows you very well
He stands on your shoulder chipping away
Until the day . . .

That there's nothing left
The day of your death
But until that day
He still chips away
Chipping, chipping and *chipping!*

He never stops
Until you pop
Eating at your head
Until you're *dead!*

Raj Patel (12)
St Andrew's CE High School for Boys, Worthing

A Human Horror

He stands alone
Staring
Not blinking or moving
Just staring.

His eyes follow you
Invisible against his dark clothes and mask
He hovers above you, behind you, in front of you
And when you turn the corner, he is already there

Eventually he lifts his hand
He holds the side of his mask and pulls
What you see then is the only thing to fear
You see fear itself reflected in his white, white face.

Zach de Vries (12)
St Andrews CE School for Boys, Worthing

Football

Football is cool
Football is great
We play down the park
Me and my mate.

Kicking it about
At the neighbour's wall
It's a really great game
The game of football.

One day I wish
I could be a pro
I've got the talent
I just need to show.

It would be amazing
I would have all the gear
I can hear it now
The sound of the crowd cheer!

Jonathan Hibbs (14)
St Andrew's CE High School for Boys, Worthing

Money

It was a good creation
Turned evil by man
Greed took over and everything got out of hand
People die, people cry and people feel pain
All because of man's need to gain
Money is power
And power is money
But after all money is just funny.

Alex Kelly (14)
St Andrew's CE High School for Boys, Worthing

We Can Help Them

I look from the heavens down into the slums
Where food and drink are only for some
How do they survive without TV? I think
But we can't imagine three days with no drink.

Yet, without them chocolate would be no more
While we look from the place where big birds soar
And I can't imagine earning under the minimum wage
Yet we all ignore it and turn over the page.

Caught in a trap, there's no way out
Yet Heaven's help gets sucked up the spout
They knock on the door again and again, but what do we do?
Give them the money, we cannot say 'shoo'.

Who are these people I hear you say
They cannot be human, yet they live by day
They are amongst us, is my reply
On our very planet, yet you say 'why'?
We can help them and give them a hand
Come and join me and dig them out of the sand.

Jack Stuart (13)
St Andrew's CE High School for Boys, Worthing

Boredom

Boredom comes and goes through lessons and woes
Lives in the school
Under crooked floorboards
Floating and crawling around, invisible to the eye
Attracted to passes in the dull corridors
Sliming under doors and jumping through walls
Creeping on children, all ages and sizes
Watch out for the *boredom monster!*

Matthew Harrison (13)
St Andrew's CE High School for Boys, Worthing

New Year, New You

Drop the unhealthy foods
Drop the jean size to look fab
Tone up those sloppy abs
The media tells us we must be slim
It should be a way of life, not just a whim
We can achieve this impossible task
How can we? I hear you ask
Get out and walk
Don't sit and talk
Do that ten mile run
You never know, it might be fun!
You haven't finished yet
There's not enough sweat
Pump that iron for bigger biceps
Push up and down to improve your triceps
You may end up sore
But you've got to do more
Run up a hill
Or get on a treadmill
Turn your flab
Into some abs
Get fit
Don't sit
And never quit
If all that fails
Never forget the nip and tuck
Or even a bit of lipo-suck.

Jack Salter (13)
St Andrew's CE High School for Boys, Worthing

Top Gear

Richard Hammond with his white teeth
Clarkson is tall and the Hamster so small
Stig punishing every car in the world
James May being an English posh gentleman
Star in the reasonably priced car won by an English hero.

Fights on the cool wall
Hamster eating pictures of the German and Japanese cars
A special place is reserved for an English icon the Aston Martin.

News from all car makers
The powerboard too tall for Hammond.

Marcus Hoare (13)
St Andrew's CE High School for Boys, Worthing

Cats

She's fat and round
Just lies on the ground
And does nothing at all
Until you get the mouse
Then she'll play around
Running up and down the hall.

Round, round she will run
Enjoying all the lovely fun
She rolls around on the floor
And has a little crawl
But when she's done
With all the fun
She's exhausted, fat and round
She's had enough, wants no more
And collapses right there on the ground!

Ben Harvey (13)
St Andrew's CE High School for Boys, Worthing

One Thing

There is one thing about poetry
That doesn't just slip into the head
The way you must think
Stays with you from breakfast to bed.

So writing a poem is hard
And so must be seen as a choice
Rather than being forced to
So we can choose, have a voice.

Potentially line one is the hardest
For a constant struggle to be inspired
Then there is the ending
But the end result, by all is aspired.

Lawrence Job (14)
St Andrew's CE High School for Boys, Worthing

The Sloth

On one fine Saturday
I went to a great party
When I arrived they all said, 'Hey!'
And I said, 'Whey!'
I saw quite a lot of my mates
They all came dressed as pirates.
But there was one kid
He was a bit of a div
And he came dressed as a sloth!

Tom Setterfield (14)
St Andrew's CE High School for Boys, Worthing

Love/Lust

Love is a pain that doesn't hurt
Lust is lying in the gutter, hitting the dirt
Love wears a rainbow, beautiful, free
Lust lies naked, fixated on she
Love flows loose, disengaged
Lust is in chains, its pride upstaged
Love ascends, higher and higher
Lust falls down with its obsessive desire
Love sings proud of itself
Lust remains introverted, buried in itself
Love takes you on its back, tears you away
Lust devours you, leaves you falling away.

Simon Tarbet (13)
St Andrew's CE High School for Boys, Worthing

The Night Sky

I look up
Into a black alien world
A million stars flung out
Across the void of space
Tiny twinkles of light
From a distant, unknown world
A large disk of grey
So close and yet so far
The moon, a cratered friend
I long to be out there
Mars winks to me from the heavens
A tiny orange in an abyss
That does not see me
Staring up into the night sky.

James Fyles (14)
St Andrew's CE High School for Boys, Worthing

Waking Up

I wake up in the morning looking a mess
But right now I couldn't care less
My eyes are still heavy
I can't get up
On my bedside table there sits a cup
There is my mother telling me
She brought me up a cup of tea.

I slowly wake, get out of bed
Sit up and rub my head
The sun is shining in my eye
I bend over to get my tie.

I get dressed to look my best
Walk out the door to leave my nest
This is how I wake up.

Sam Cleife (14)
St Andrew's CE High School for Boys, Worthing

Untitled

School is so boring
I'm surprised we aren't all snoring
School is as bad as an infection or scab
Just like Worthing to Scotland by cab
School is like reading tax law
What a big, big snore
When the next lesson comes there is a moan
We all can't wait till we get home.

Adam Keet (13)
St Andrew's CE High School for Boys, Worthing

The Match

Shoulder to shoulder we enter the ground
A sea of red and green milling around
The atmosphere excited and tense
After all, it's the final event.

Surrounded by the smell of burgers and beer
The long awaited teams finally appear
The crowd erupt in a huge great cheer
The moment we have all waited for is here.

The game starts with a whistle blow
We all hope our team puts on a good show
The players clash in a steaming scrum
Reds grab the ball and begin to run.

The crowd gives off a mighty roar
As they head to the line for the first score
We watch our player take the kick
It shaves the post and we all feel sick.

The whistle blows for half-time
And only one team has crossed the line
Time for a quick refreshment dash
Then the teams return for another clash.

The second-half for the reds goes wrong
The greens have come back very strong
Two quick tries are scored by them
Giving them a score of ten.

With all their strength the reds attack
But fail to hold the green team back
As the final whistle blows
Our hearts and hopes sink down to our toes.

Daniel Long (13)
St Andrew's CE High School for Boys, Worthing

Cartoons

Comical, funny and insane
Full of colour and bright characters
Cartoons are great
So many and more to come.

Mickey Mouse a brightly coloured mouse
With yellow shoes
And bright red trousers
With buttons, white.

The naughty American Simpsons
Yellow and funny
Created by one
Carried on by all.

For we all like a good cartoon
Funny with all new jokes and gags
Colours we find amazing
Worlds we have never seen.

Clip after clip filmed
In many different ways
Step by step clay animation
Or straight drawn, how we like

The wondrous imaginations we have
Now we have cartoons we can adore

Animation is just brilliant
And we love them so
So why not watch them
And create them.

For we all like a good laugh
And that's what they do
What are they?
Cartoons.

Ian Ifield (13)
St Andrew's CE High School for Boys, Worthing

My Basketball Poem

Basketball, oh basketball
I hit it against the wall
Basketball, oh basketball
There's only one kind.

I play every day
Even when I'm away
In Australia
Or in the USA!

The teams all array
Who compete and play
The skills are many
Even some are quite funny.

Some day, maybe
I'd like to be
A pro
Well, that'd be a dream.

Basketball, oh basketball
Oh, it's my favourite sport
Basketball, oh basketball
You can all play, even if you're short!

Dan Edmunds (14)
St Andrew's CE High School for Boys, Worthing

Hate

Hate
A black cloud floating eerily about the shadows
Marching to war and death
In the heart of all men
You cannot get rid of me
I destroy lives
People fight me but cannot beat me
I know no limits
I speak to your conscience
Hate.

Thomas Chambers (12)
St Andrew's CE High School for Boys, Worthing

The Romans Came A-Marching

The Romans came a-marching across the lush green grass
The Romans came a-marching, silver swords and shields of brass
The Roman's spears came soaring across the blood-red sky
The Roman horses came charging, swords held up high
The Britons' front rank was smashed
Their rear rank reduced to mash
The Britons began to run
The Romans showed no mercy.

Thomas Barrett (14)
St Andrew's CE High School for Boys, Worthing

Man

One thousand trees standing tall
A roof of leaves covers all
A long blue river flows down the hill
All is quiet, all is still.

Birds soar freely through the sky
There is no stealing and no one lies
Clouds float by when they please
All is good, all is free.

Where the waters meet the land
Waves fall over yellow sands
Mountains tall and valleys deep
All will stay, all will keep.

Then one day the winds grow strong
Something's happened, something's wrong
The sky turns dark and the trees they fall
The sea starts rising and engulfs all.

Creatures come and steal the land
They start off small but then expand
They do all this because they can
These creatures that are known as Man.

David Bennett (13)
St Andrew's CE High School for Boys, Worthing

Hate

I lurk in your body
I sneak around your blood
Your body's like a lobby
To me when I escape.

I wear purple, orange or red
Depending what I'm like
Sometimes you think I'm dead
But I'm just waiting for a fight.

I say hurtful things
Like 'stupid', 'dolt head' and 'fat'
I can play you like strings
I hit people like a bat.

I sneak, I creep and I crawl
To all points, north and south
After I use them you'll want to wear a shawl
But I'll explode out of your mouth.

When I'm active
I'll never stop to rest
When I'm done I go through a sieve
Till I'm a tiny seed waiting till I become my best.

Zoom, broom, bash, crash
I knock into your blood cells
If they see me they're gone in a flash
But if they don't, then they're in Hell.

James Wickett (12)
St Andrew's CE High School for Boys, Worthing

Autumn - Haiku

The falling red leaves
The natural mild weather
The calm autumn peace.

William Hayward (13)
St Andrew's CE High School for Boys, Worthing

Lost

Confused
Reserved
Derived

I wander through the unknown passage
I do not know my way
Silhouettes in the half-moon light
I don't know what to say.

Unsure
Unfound
Terrified

In the darkness I wonder
I'm unsure where to go
I don't know what I have to do
There's nothing left to know.

Hidden
Ridden
Vulnerable

I feel like I am naked
Nothing to defend
I am a little child
I only need a friend.

George Foden (13)
St Andrew's CE High School for Boys, Worthing

Love

Love is an illusion of sex and adoration
It goes on forever like constipation
You push it harder to get it out of your system
But you know it will go on until you break
And when it goes away, you feel lost and empty
That is the time when you go searching for *more*
That is the vicious cycle of *love*.

James Bryer (12)
St Andrew's CE High School for Boys, Worthing

Depression

All alone and standing still
Not moving
From the ground beside the grave
The Earth
Never moving
As tears of sorrow and sadness fall onto his black shirt
The soft silenced cries of his broken life, break the silence
As the spirit of the lost soul
Cries out to the boy,
'Save happiness in your life and be free
Enjoy your time on the Earth
For I will never forget you
You will always be my son and I will always love you
And our lost spirits will be reunited one day
Until that day comes
Farewell my son.'
As the boy wipes his tears
And as the Earth is standing still
He picks a rose from a nearby bush
The only tear manages to seep into the petals
And as he leaves he takes one last look at the grave
And throws the rose over his shoulder and onto the grave
Proving the love
The care
And the bonding in which they share
Proving that the two will never be separated apart
Proving that they will always be in each other's hearts
Proving they will never be forgotten
And that love
Really does exist.

Jonty Lockyer (13)
St Andrew's CE High School for Boys, Worthing

Pain

A ghost, invisible, blown about in the midnight gale
Death, his plan, draped in pain, but with no trail
Like a ripple of water on the stream of death
The quiet steps on the soil of the battlefield
Of the forgotten souls.

Draped in the hide of the black demons
He screams, 'Mercy unto me!'
With the ominous blood running down him
He fights for the survival of his own mind.

Matthew Badcock (12)
St Andrew's CE High School for Boys, Worthing

Compassion

I feel it inside me
It drapes in blossomey-red, a spring rose
It glides like a ghost in the mist
They are going nowhere, but always somewhere
It speaks to me, like a voice in my mind
Growing, getting stronger and stronger.

I feel it all around me
They're a beautiful red rose
Easily broken, hard to fix
It goes where it wants
Moves the way it feels
It tells you how it feels.

It's in everyone I see.

Jamie Shiel (13)
St Andrew's CE High School for Boys, Worthing

Hate

I'm wearing hate
I get pulled around and around
I'm lost in my fate.

I'm feeling disgust
I'm being back-stabbed
I've lost all my trust.

Laurence Pengelly (12)
St Andrew's CE High School for Boys, Worthing

Hate

Dark and black
Walking down the street
Black tie
Black suit
Red eyes
Swift and silent
Through war and anger
Sometimes discreet
Sometimes obvious,
'Stop, get out!'
'I hate you!'
'No!'
Cold like the wind
Hot, the sun
Loud
Quiet
Light
Annoying
Dark and black.

Chris Candy (12)
St Andrew's CE High School for Boys, Worthing

Love

Love is the feeling that lasts forever
Love is the feeling that brings us together
Love is when two minds unite
Love is when you can't sleep at night
Love is the feeling that complicates our life
Love is the feeling that pulls you through strife
Love is where you can't bear to be apart
Love is where you communicate through the heart
Love is the feeling that goes on through your mind
Love is the feeling that defines mankind
Love is why the world was invented
Love is why we feel so repentant
Love is the feeling that lasts forever
Love is the feeling that brings us together.

Jake Stoddart (12)
St Andrew's CE High School for Boys, Worthing

Hate

Hate is all around us
Hate is everywhere
Breaking out of you
Like a bullet from a gun
Doing something unexpected
Doing something wrong.

Hate lives in the fists of man
And makes you lose your pride
He doesn't have to move
He doesn't have to talk
He gets his point across
This is how he does his job.

Sam Joyce (13)
St Andrew's CE High School for Boys, Worthing

Madness

Madness is mad
As you probably guessed
He can be as nutty as a fruitcake
At his very best.

He stalks after grannies
And drinks from the loo
His favourite meal is psychopaths
Covered in melted poo.

Now if you meet this man, beware
For his pupils of craziness are everywhere
If you don't want to be one of them, leave them alone
But if you do, you'll end up in a mental home.

Harvey Heasman (12)
St Andrew's CE High School for Boys, Worthing

Hate

If you ever meet me
You better watch out
I ruin people's lives
And kill others wives
I wander in the darkness
Waiting to pounce
I wear my red cloak all day
Ready to grab my prey
If you see me you should run
You may hurt someone
If I get you
And you wouldn't have a clue.

Ryan Gangloff (12)
St Andrew's CE High School for Boys, Worthing

Fear

Fear is the one who hid at the back
Sitting
Alone
Dark and mysterious
Shrouded in hate
Scared
Afraid.

Josh Fox (12)
St Andrew's CE High School for Boys, Worthing

Winter's Perfect Friend

On a cold wet day we need something warm
A coat, a hot cup of tea, anything
And when it snows we need a friend to play with
But when we need help and no one is there
We need a friend on a cold winter's day
Someone to look after us as we do to them.

A friendship is fragile
It is hard to find a good friend
Easy to change them
And difficult to forget them.

Appreciate your friend and never forget
The good times
The bad times
And the fun times
Because every time you are with your friend
You will feel safe on a cold winter's day.

Don't use your friend
If there are things you do not like
Look behind them
There is always a special part
Try to find it.

Winter's perfect friend is always somewhere.

Emily Williams (14)
St Mary's Hall School, Brighton

Child Abuse

I'm called Georgia, I'm three years old
My eyes are sore, so I cannot see
I must be dumb, I must be bad
What else would make my daddy so mad?
I wish I was better, I wish I wasn't ugly
Then maybe my mummy would want to hug me again.

I cannot talk or say a word
I can't be naughty otherwise I'm locked up all day
When I wake up I'm alone
And the house is dark, my parents aren't home.

When my mummy finally comes
I'll try to be good and nice
But I'll still get whipped tonight
Don't make a sound, I just heard a car.

My daddy is back from the pub
I can hear him curse, he calls my name
I press myself against a wall, I try to hide

But I'm so terrified, I start to cry
He finds me at last
He shouts and says it's all my fault
That he suffers at work
He kicks and hits me and yells some more

I finally get free and run for the door
But he's already locked it
He throws me against a wall
And pushes me down the stairs
I fall, my bones almost broken,
'I'm sorry,' I scream, but it's too late
Oh please God have mercy, oh please let it end.

And my daddy stops and heads for the door
While I lay on the floor
I'm only three
And my daddy murdered me.

Emma Burgess (13)
St Mary's Hall School, Brighton

Turn Back Time

If I could turn back time I would . . .
See your smile again
Hear one of your awful jokes again
Watch your eyes when you were excited again.

If I could turn back time I would . . .
See you cry of happiness again
Hear your laugh again
Watch you play with your Barbie's again.

If I could turn back time I would . . .
See you doing your hair to perfection like you did every morning again
Hear you gossiping to your friends again
Watch you playing on the swings again.

I wish I never had to find you lying there in the road
I wish I could see you again at least one more time
I wish I could get the sound of your scream and the car hitting you
I wish I could get the image of the car running you over out of my mind.

Ciara McGrath (13)
St Mary's Hall School, Brighton

Fake Love

'I love you,'   he says.
But I can't feel   a thing. Isn't
It meant to hit you,   and your heart
Starts beating like it never has before?
'I love you too,' comes my emotionless
Reply, coated in icy-cold water. We
Hug, we kiss, we touch, all so deep
And meaningful, but I can't feel;
A thing. I am cold and motion-
Less inside and I know
If he can't save me
Nothing can.
Ever.

Freya-Rose Tanner (14)
St Mary's Hall School, Brighton

World War II Wishing Wings

If I had wings I would fly out of this hell
I can just imagine how the wonderful feelings would swell up inside me
To be free once more
Dreams are lined up outside the door just waiting to be picked
Deep within my soul I am shallow and I hear a beating call
But within I am small
As the days go on I realise that if I wish hard enough my dream
I can pursue
But one fateful day I went into that room
It filled up with gas and now I am no more.

Jasmine Kilpatrick (12)
St Mary's Hall School, Brighton

Through Your Eyes

I see what you see and I don't like it
I know what you mean when you see no light
I wish I could show you how sorry I am
But you've heard that before.

I want you to know how hard it is
I just want you to understand
Is it changing a habit or changing a person?

If you knew how it is, would you understand?
If it could not change, could you accept it?
If only I could show you.

My heart sinks when I know I let you down
I try my hardest not to forget
I try to live without just to calm your anger
But no, it is too late, you are already crying.

I begin to hate myself as if I was two people
I punish myself when I feel
Just in case it will let you into my world
For a second.

Julia Hollis (14)
St Mary's Hall School, Brighton

Special Place

There is a place where I like to go
A place where I am free
A place where I can be myself
Where no one else can see me
I can feel what I want
I can see what I want.

This special place where I like to go
It isn't by the sea
It's not in the woods
Or on a hill
It's somewhere that can't be found
For this special place is me.

Holly Welsh (14)
St Mary's Hall School, Brighton

Through The Eyes Of . . .

Rolling forward in this machine
I look outside, not much to be seen
All the same colours, dull and grey
Not much excitement in my day
I stop at a street and walk up the path
Not much here, to make me laugh
The houses all packed tightly and narrow
I don't think I'd notice if I was shot with an arrow
I reach a house at the end of the street
I kick the door twice with my feet
It is opened quite wide, I'm not greeted at all
I get into bed, I feel like a fool
I dream of great things, exciting and bright
And wake up very tired to the morning light
A new day begins, I guess that's a shame
Because I know it'll all end the same.

Nina Sarfas (14)
St Mary's Hall School, Brighton

Wondering

I lay on my bed wondering where you are
What you're doing, have you gone far?
The tears on my pillow have all dried now
I'm wondering why, I'm wondering how
How the stains of our hatred have just disappeared
How the proof of my love has suddenly cleared
What's the point of my life as depression runs rife?
There's a knock on the door, I wonder who it's for
I wonder if it's you, I hope this wish comes true.

Esme Sarfas (14)
St Mary's Hall School, Brighton

Sisters

The car pulled up and she'd arrived
A curly mop and beaming smile
I looked at her unprepared
In a way I really was quite scared.

All of a sudden in my world
It wasn't just me
I wasn't the only girl.

I took my role as older sister
To always help and never leave her
Little did I know how much I'd love her.

When my world changed
And we became sisters I knew at once
Everything would be different
I did not mind the noise and mess
The dirty clothes and toys undressed.

Now I stand here older and wiser
Teenage sister with life behind us
I feel I have been given the greatest gift of love
And friendship never to be left.

Emily Pearce (14)
St Mary's Hall School, Brighton

The Well

Here I am in my well, with nobody around me
Just the mould on the walls
And the drip, drip of the water splashing onto my head
But I hear the rustle and a splash
I find that a figure has appeared in the gloom
A glimpse of light shone in my face
I noticed it was a torch held by a mysterious man
I did not know who it was but that night I was saved
By my guardian angel.

Romina Duplain (11)
St Mary's Hall School, Brighton

Poem On Frankie The Pencil Case

The day I got forgotten
I was scared from top to bottom
I was on my own
And I forgot my mobile phone
When the Turner beast came in
I thought I was to go in the bin
When she picked me up in the air
Oh, how I got a scare
Now I wanted to cry
For I was certain I was to die
She put me in a dark hole
No one was there, not even a mole
The next morning a hero took me out
And at that moment I was up and about
Hero Quantick took me back
And once again I was in my lovely sack.

Sophie Mitchell (12)
St Mary's Hall School, Brighton

The Lonely Willow Tree

The tree in the forest all alone
Never ever moaned
He cried inside
With so much pride
But the other old willows knew
When the wind blew
And it began to rain
They knew where it came
From that lonely old willow tree again.

Zaynah Al-Shamkhani (11)
St Mary's Hall School, Brighton

Untitled

You led me in
Treated me as one of the rest
Made me feel unique
Cherished, cared and protected me
When I finally adapted
You showed me who you really were
Late at night, you came
Strolling in smiling
Laying on my bed, I felt your warm smile touch my heart
As I began to tell you my thoughts
Your hand crept closer and closer
Closing in on me
I felt your cold, mysterious rather different heart
My body began to tense
Now going into a deep freeze
I felt your cold unloving hand touching my breast
I now know who you really are!

Sarah Russo (13)
St Mary's Hall School, Brighton

The Kindness Of Others

When I became conscious I found myself in the middle of a war
I lay there bleeding, I wondered what my wife and children
would be doing?
All I could hear were the voices of guns and see men fighting
for their lives
A gun viciously fired and my best friend lay beside me
I tried to talk to him but he was already gone
A figure appeared out of the dust
It was a German soldier, I thought I was a dead man walking
But he reached out his hand and propped me up against the mud
Then poured water in my mouth
We heard footsteps coming and the German soldier ran off
Although I never saw this kind man again
He stayed in my memory like an old photograph
Because kindness saved me that day.

Olivia Mason (12)
St Mary's Hall School, Brighton

I Wish You Hadn't

I'm sure I used to be yours
Laughing at the people walk by
Walking down to Brighton's beachy shores
Watching the starry sky.

But do you miss me the same way?
Your eyes - they'll never see or so they say.

I wish you hadn't left me here
You know I'm all alone
Look - there comes another tear
Another crying moan.

So maybe I'll join you
On the other side
Our love - so true
Nothing to hide.

Ana Whittock (13)
St Mary's Hall School, Brighton

The Once Running Fox

When morning comes with dew on grass
Robins sing sweet tunes that last
There comes a horn with a thousand barks
That scare away the lonely larks.

A fair bright light from the rising sun
The fox all day must run, run, run
Across the fields the horses play
Till they catch the fox, they'll hunt all day.

With nose to ground, they'll not repent
For now they have the fox's scent
The bark, the gallop, the once running fox
The hunt has come to an awful stop.

A great crowd gathers, they all cheer and laugh
As an exhausted fox is torn apart
And in the evening, by faded light
A vixen looks through the dreary night.

Charlotte Patching (12)
St Mary's Hall School, Brighton

An African Orphan

I lie still each night and day
Praying a Samaritan will pass my way
The sun shines down on the imaginary lake
I want to play but all over I ache
There is no water, no rain
I look up to the windowpane
Nothing there, not even a drip
I can taste on my lip
My bones are string, my skin like foil
I can't move, cannot speak, just curled like a coil
For this is my life
Why not just hand me the knife?

Sophie Ebeling (13)
St Mary's Hall School, Brighton

You Know You Shouldn't

You know you shouldn't
But maybe you should
Just one
Or two
Mum will never know.

They look so tasty
Covered in sugar
Small, big
Sweet, sour
You're itching to try.

You have done it now
Mum is going to shout
Oh no
Not good
You didn't mean to.

The jar is empty
Mum's home in one hour
This is very bad
You better buy more.

Now Mum has come home
You go say, 'Hello
Hi Mum.'
'Hello.'
It is all right.

Mum goes to the jar
She looks inside
She looks
Then smiles
She knows what you did.

Lily Oakley (12)
St Mary's Hall School, Brighton

Those Big Black Eyes

I look at this painting of two children
I am scared at what I have seen
Their eyes look longingly at you
And follow you everywhere you go
The little boy has a slight smile
But to only lure you in
To those big black eyes.

Their pale faces, their long faces
Are daunting and distressing
The little boy is pointing
At what? I do not know
The little girl has a slight smile
But only to lure you in
To those big black eyes.

The boy's tall black hat
The girl's blue flowery bonnet
Make the children's faces paler
And brings out the colour in their clothes
The hats are different but have the same shape
But only to lure you in
To those big black eyes.

The horse on which they sit upon
Is standing longingly on the ground
Maybe it is the weight on his back
Or maybe he is cold
But looks like a humble and kind horse
But only to lure you in
To those big black eyes.

Evie Pattenden (12)
St Mary's Hall School, Brighton

One Last Day Till She Moves Away

It's the last day I get till she moves away
It's the one day I get so I mustn't regret
It's the last day I get so I will not forget.
Twelve years have passed in each other's company
So much has happened, good and bad
What can I say as she moves away?

Arriving at the destination that I most fear
Talking to the person that means the world to me
So many memories rushing through our heads
The day she came round my house for a two night sleepover
We cycled down to the park and got called gotchic by two French girls
The Saturdays we sat in my wooden box reading magazines
And stuffing our faces with Haribo! What a laugh we had.

It's time to say goodbye now
But it will be OK
I can write to her every day
Oh no, I can't do this, my eyes are starting to water
I can't hold it in
I can't hold it in
I won't hold it in
I won't hold it in
I have to say goodbye . . .

It's been over a year since she left
I haven't written for months
I miss her so much!
I need to write more so that's what I will do
This friendship is not going to waste
It's the last chance I get, so I mustn't forget!

Yzzy Lancaster (13)
St Mary's Hall School, Brighton

War

I hear the planes drumming overhead
Their heavy deadly load waiting to kill
The sirens start their screeching
They drive me mad, I hear it every night
It's telling us to get to safety
The humming of the planes and the screaming of the sirens
Fills my heart with fear.

I sit in the shelter
Are my dad and brother dead in the trenches rotting
Or are they still fighting on bravely, still thinking of us back at home?
Have they lost any of their friends?
Do they think of us or have they forgotten us?
They haven't been home for eight months
We haven't heard from them for two months
But we also haven't got the letter everybody dreads.

We were in the shelter all night
It's morning, as if no war is happening
No houses bombs, no one crying because they got a letter
No one except for my mother and me
My father and brother, dead
I hate this
I would kill myself to bring just one of them back.

I remember last Christmas I got a doll
It broke so Father spent all day fixing it
And how proud we were of them for signing up
My brother only 16, stupid boy, now he's dead, he shouldn't
have been there
My father was too old to go but he said he was 37
Now he's dead
Now it's me and mother left.

Amy Martin (13)
St Mary's Hall School, Brighton

Rainforest

A man bought himself a lovely painting
Of a very pretty green rainforest
Because he liked them so much

The picture hung on the wall in the living room
Displayed high up, so everyone could see it

He loved this pretty picture
But had to leave it at home
He was off on a long holiday but to come back soon.

When he came back two months later
He was scared to find the picture had been ruined

The trees and flowers, animals and plants
Had all disappeared and only land was left

A few months went by and he started to notice
The picture on the wall getting smaller and smaller

Soon there was barely anything left
He called the shop and they said
They didn't know what had happened

He turned on the news and surprisingly found
The picture was doing what was really happening

He was so upset his picture was going
And so were the rainforests, going, going, going.

Rosie Moss (12)
St Mary's Hall School, Brighton

A Waterfall

A waterfall seems tall and proud
It rushes to the bottom and lands with a splash
It explodes on the rocks like a water bomb
A waterfall plunges to the plunge pool.

It starts as a stream and suddenly it smashes on the rocks
It noisily goes over the edge and showers the rocks, heavily
The water is powerful and fast
It gushes and rushes and hits the rocks
It flows rapidly over the edge like a water bomb.

Stephanie Robb (13)
St Mary's Hall School, Brighton

What Is It Like?

What is it like to be blind?
To never see the world
To never see the beautiful sunset
To never see the countryside in the morning?

What is it like to be deaf?
To never hear a baby cry
To never hear the sweet sound of music
To see a little bird, but to never hear it sing?

What is it like to be dumb?
To never sing a note
To never talk to anyone like you and me
To never say I love you?

How should I know?
I'm one of the lucky ones.

Angela Needham (14)
St Mary's Hall School, Brighton

The Dark Alley

Through the darkness he came creeping
With the gun grasped in his hands
I hear a shot and then I feel cold
I look down and see red
My life has surely come to an end.

In the alley where a life was lost
A child wandered in, cold and scared
He saw a figure come out of the shadows
Holding a lump of cold metal
He heard a bang and then nothing more.

Three years on from the death
An old woman walks into the alley
As she walks on she feels a pain
Like she's never felt before
She's dead before she hits the ground.

Ben Byrne (12)
St Paul's Catholic College, Burgess Hill

Dreaded War

Shells bombarding the brave soldiers
Fierce deadly gunshots heard everywhere
Brave soldiers, fighting for their country
Helplessly dying in No-Man's-Land
Bang, bang, blood, blood
All you need to tell the story.

More and more courageous soldiers die
Shot, bombed, maybe even in the eye
Now only a couple of soldiers alive
Painfully fighting for their country
Bang, bang, blood, blood
All you need to tell the story.

Mina Fidal (11)
St Paul's Catholic College, Burgess Hill

Poor Helpless Soldiers

Fierce soldiers bleed helplessly
Final prayers choke in pain
Explosions make the soldiers duck
Thundering trenches choke sadly
Muddy soldiers bleed suddenly
Rotten boots stumble and break.

Tom Ward (12)
St Paul's Catholic College, Burgess Hill

I Walk, I Run, I Stop And . . . I'm Gone

I walk
Silently through the forgotten world
Trees are reaching out for me
And still
I walk.

I run
Spinning faces tormenting my soul
Dashing figures circling my path
And still
I run.

I stop
There's voices echoing in my mind
There's shadows watching my every step - waiting
Watching . . .
And still
I stop.

I'm gone
There's screaming of a distant voice
Daggers tearing through my body
Piercing, tear
I'm gone.

Brontë McDonald (12)
St Paul's Catholic College, Burgess Hill

The Mysterious Woods!

The dark creepy wood
Was where I was walking through
What was there to do?

All alone in the darkness
Anything could happen
What could happen now?

What's that in the trees?
I start to hear strange noises
I am really scared!

What was that I saw?
It was moving in the trees
It tried to grab me!

What is going on?
I couldn't see anything
I could just hear it!

I was petrified
It's never happened before
I run home screaming . . . !

Jasmine Guerrero (12)
St Paul's Catholic College, Burgess Hill

All Or Nothing

Above us the war is fierce
Below us it is silent
Inside us it is painful
Outside us it is life
Over us it is madness
Under us it is sadness
With us there is all hope
Without us there is nothing.

Jessica Bennett (12)
St Paul's Catholic College, Burgess Hill

Where Am I?

In a dark alleyway
I see a man
He's all in black
I stop
I stare
I scream
I run
And run, and run
A car
Crash, bang, scream
I open my eyes
It is so bright
Where am I?
I stood up
I see a man
A different one
I run
He calls my name
I stop and turn
Who are you?
Hannah, it's me, God
I look up
There's an angel above
Is this a dream
Or am I dead?

Hannah Brown (13)
St Paul's Catholic College, Burgess Hill

Through The Fog

Through the thick fog we could see an active bomb
Under extreme pressure we carried on
In the distance we could see the allies
Over the top we saw planes shooting at something in the distance
Under our feet with every step could be a bomb
But all I feel is madness.

George Francis (11)
St Paul's Catholic College, Burgess Hill

Home Alone

I lay in bed all alone
All silent until I hear the ringing of the phone
I was not to go
I was underaged now and I couldn't let anyone know
The phone calmed and I lay shivering in bed
Wondering when Mum would get back from her date with Ned
But I knew she'd take as long as possible
Knock, knock, knock, the sound came echoing up from the hall
I breathed slowly now petrified, but I stayed for Mum
However the noise didn't stop, it banged louder through my eardrum
I tried to stay calm but it carried on like an alarm
I tiptoed out of my room to look at the present
But my sight was not at all pleasant
Now *all* doors banging, closing me in
I was trapped crying, I felt as small and humble as a pin
Soon doors would open, what *should I do?*

Lucy Hardy (12)
St Paul's Catholic College, Burgess Hill

World War I

The soldiers had to be prepared
But they were very scared
There was blood everywhere
And there was mud on their boots.

They're crying out tears
Looking at the people that have died
Whilst their family
Are hoping they have survived.

They just hope that the war can just end
So they can go home and be in peace again
They were fighting for their lives and their country
Hoping they could go home and be a saviour.

Isobel Cowan (11)
St Paul's Catholic College, Burgess Hill

The Tell-Tale Heart

The groaning of the floorboards under my feet
It sounds like zombies and it makes your heart beat
You're wondering what's under there that makes you shiver
Well, I will tell you this, it makes you scared and quiver
I pulled up the floorboards to reveal
And then I saw it, my nightmare was real
I looked in his eyes, they were pale white
He sat up slowly and gave me a fright
I ran to my shed to get my saw
I cut off his head and now he wants more
It's running after me, I'm dead for sure.

Rory Gillespie (12)
St Paul's Catholic College, Burgess Hill

It

In the bedroom
On the stair
A brutal gloom
With an evil glare.

Someone stood there
Dressed in black
Long fair hair
Swooped down its back.

Its fingers thin
And red with blood
A cold black sin
A violent thud.

It came to me
In a glow of black
It had the key
So I could never come back.

Ellie Wilding (12)
St Paul's Catholic College, Burgess Hill

The Tell-Tale Heart

I run out the gate into the night
What was that thing? I felt it bite
I trembled with fear, I stumble and stagger
He was going to kill me and with his dagger
It was running up behind me, leaping as he went
As he gained closer, I could smell his scent
Shouting the words I dread to hear
You're going to die, I felt such fear
I lunged at him with a knife
At this moment, I was taking his life
He fell to the floor, now he was dead
His legs were floppy and so was his head
Finally I'm free, where will I go?
Now he's gone, everyone will know.

Rebecca Harvey (13)
St Paul's Catholic College, Burgess Hill

Choking

Choking
The mist is covering me
Choking me to death
A man walks over to me
I hold my breath
The man walks closer
Will I survive?
Behind me is a river
I have to dive . . .

The water is covering me
Drowning me to death
A crocodile swims over to me
I'm losing my breath
The crocodile comes closer
Will I survive?
I try to get out of the river
I slip and die.

Arron Barnett (12)
St Paul's Catholic College, Burgess Hill

I'm Running and Trying To Get Away

I'm running and trying to get away
Lying and trying not to sleep
Sleeping and trying to hide my fear
I'm running and trying to get away.

I'm sleeping and hoping the dream will stop
Crouching and hoping it'll not come
It's coming and I'm hoping it will not see me
I'm sleeping and hoping the dream will stop.

I'm hiding and dreading what'll happen next
Closing my eyes and dreading the scream
Clenching my fists and dreading the moment
I'm hiding and dreading what'll happen next.

I'm running and trying to get away
Lying and trying not to sleep
Sleeping and trying to hide my fear
I'm running and trying to get away.

Amy Altenberg (12)
St Paul's Catholic College, Burgess Hill

No-Man's-Land

Blood, rats, beetles and soil
Bombshells, bullets and gore
The Allies and Germans fighting for their country
Who is going to win?

Skies full of darkness and planes
Pigeons and horses moving on
Drooping trees and crippled bushes
Thick slushy mud and bodies.

Letters home of bedraggled soldiers
Wispy bandages wrapped around arms
Nervous wives, praying prayers
Children hoping, 'Daddy won't get
Trench Foot, will he?'

Catherine Eckford (12)
St Paul's Catholic College, Burgess Hill

The Mysterious Man

Whatever it is I'm not scared
Whatever it is I'm not quite sane
Whatever it is it gave me a scare
Whatever I am
Not quite sure
Whatever I am going to do laying in the garden I chew
Whatever it is I'm not scared
Whatever it is I'm not quite sure
Whatever it is I'm not scared but then it gave me a scare
I scream
Don't know who it is
It might be a man or a can banging
Whatever it is it gave me a scare
This time I'm not quite sure
Whatever it is I'm going to be dead.

Ciara Hunt (13)
St Paul's Catholic College, Burgess Hill

The Beast Within

Twist the bones and bend the back
Stick the nails in his fat
The moon around will change his fate
Like the wolf he now will hate
He will change on moon a-full
Like the tides that do pull
The howls and hunger in him will grow
He'll want to taste flesh and bones
The werewolf's howl he answers thus
The claws and jaws become he must
The words of the wild
The words of the weird
The words of the werewolf in his ears.

Albert Shiell (13)
St Paul's Catholic College, Burgess Hill

Untitled

In the trenches bodies lie
Not many are breathing
The sun is high
Lice in their hair
And cuts on their skin
Some don't have the heart to do
Someone in
'Come on boys,' a sergeant says
'We won't be here for many more days.'
But it isn't as easy as everyone says
Some kneel on their knees and cry
Wait for the days to go by.

'Come on,' the sergeant says,
'We won't be here for many more days
We won't be here for many more days.'

Olympia Schoepe (12)
St Paul's Catholic College, Burgess Hill

The Chase!

Argh!
The door slammed
The man ran
His heart pumping
His legs shaking
His eyes came out with fear
He couldn't feel his fingers.

The shadow came closer and closer
He knew he was being followed
But who?
Who was after him?

Then a scream.
'Argh!'
The man no longer in sight.

William Jex (13)
St Paul's Catholic College, Burgess Hill

Courageous Soldiers

Wailing soldiers bleed helplessly
Fierce shells explode dangerously
Rotten boots trudge sorely
Courageous soldiers trudge bravely

Thundering death bleed painfully
Courageous prayers written bravely
Thundering guns shoot helplessly
Courageous soldiers trudge bravely

Prayers said, words spoken
Guns leading, people woken
Feeling sad, missing home
People feeling so alone

Courageous soldiers trudge bravely.

Emma Orlando (12)
St Paul's Catholic College, Burgess Hill

The Forest

I walked through the deep dark wood
The wind whirled around me where I stood
Bushes rustled around me
Evil shadows under the oak tree.

Something held me
A hand over my mouth to silence me
I shut my eyes tight
My heart beating with fright.

They were taking me somewhere
Who are they, who are they?
Their hands were hurting me
Who are they, who are they?
I would never open my eyes again.

Laurie Jacobs (12)
St Paul's Catholic College, Burgess Hill

A Grown Man's Tears

As we trudged through the trenches
The cold harsh wind swiping past our ears
How I so wish we could go and pull up a few beers
When we return from the land I think quietly
As I listen carefully I hear the boy's tears, just a young lad
He was pulled out from his family, his home, everything he had
Sometimes I think to myself harsh and bitter thoughts
I think, *what am I doing here, is it all my fault?*

I hear a man's tears this time
As a young lad myself, it is hard to bear
Seeing another boy cry I can do, but not a full-grown man
I cannot bear his manly tears and groans
It always hits me straight in the heart
Suddenly, I remember my dad
All the fun we had
Then his tears.

Don't cry Papa, Momma is gonna be all right
Please don't go Papa, I promise I'll be better
Mamma still loves ya, Papa please don't go.

Del Woodward (12)
St Paul's Catholic College, Burgess Hill

World War I Poem

Through the soldiers I can see a fierce group of people
That are determined to win
Through the soldiers I can see too many people dead
Who have fought with all their heart
Through the soldiers I can see people not ready to give up their lives
And are right not to
In the solders I can see too many young faces
Who are exactly like me.

Clarissa Santini (12)
St Paul's Catholic College, Burgess Hill

War Poem

Along the trench people lie
They are worried sick that they might die

Above me I can hear the planes zooming through the sky
All I want to do is sit and cry

I have fought
I am scared I might get caught

Poor ill soldiers stumble to the trench
I am holding my gun with a hard clench

I look around in despair
The world is so unfair!

Sally O'Prey (12)
St Paul's Catholic College, Burgess Hill

Poem

When there ain't no gal to kiss you
And the postman seems to miss you
And the fags have skipped an issue

When you've got an empty belly
And the bully's rotten smelly
And you're shivering like a jelly

When the Boche has done your chum in
And the sergeant's done the rum in
And there ain't no rations comin'

When the world is red and reeking
And the shrapnel shells are shrieking
And your blood is slowly leaking.

Kristoffer Andutan (11)
St Paul's Catholic College, Burgess Hill

When I Look Back

When I look back upon the war
I'll tell you all the things I saw.
Bullets and bombs shot from big guns
By the end of the day no one had won.

When I looked up and saw the foe
I feared my general would say, 'Let's go.'
Side by side we stand and fight
My comrades fall, day and night.

The general said, 'Hold your fire,'
But I couldn't hide my inner desire.
'Never give up,' I said to myself
As we stood there waiting on that muddy shelf.

We were fighting for the filthy French
Confined to living in a stinking trench.
The things I smelt made me cough and wheeze
The disgusting stench of a foul disease.

It was a wet, cold, dark, lonely night
In the middle of a desperate fight.
The flares at night lit up the sky
While bombs go off, 'I don't know why!'

To fight for your country, is it right or wrong?
In a foreign land for way too long
To kill or be killed is a waste of life
It's him or you - you don't live twice.

At the end of the war, when I come home
All these years I've been alone.
Tired and weary, yet full of pride
Only to find that my wife had died.

Matthew Delaloye (12)
St Paul's Catholic College, Burgess Hill

In The Muddy Trenches

I am in the dark muddy trenches
Below the lingering moan
During life, before death
And it's winter so I am cold
It's foggy so I can just see our fierce enemies
Straight in front of us in the distance.

Lauren Stephenson (11)
St Paul's Catholic College, Burgess Hill

Underground

Under the ground the soldiers wait
Facing a dark path of death ahead of them
Above them is a bright blue sky
But to them it's black
Before it starts they want it to end
Every one of them is there for the same reason.

Abanoub Samaan (11)
St Paul's Catholic College, Burgess Hill

Under World War I Ground

Under the ground
We hear the sound
Between our lives
They could come in with knives
We have to check around every corner, bend
Every minute could be the end
They are very fierce
They come in with knives or spears
They stabbed us in our hearts.

Dominic Marshall (11)
St Paul's Catholic College, Burgess Hill

Shells

Shells landed on brave soldiers
They tried to shoot it
Painfully they tried to stop it from exploding
None prevailed and met death
They had no prayers
To stop the deadly wailing
They limped and stumbled through bodies
We were then pinned to the trenches
They could only bleed surely
The enemies bodies were rotting away in front of me
Some say they're blind with only their arms
The thundering that came from the enemies' cannons.

James Falvey (12)
St Paul's Catholic College, Burgess Hill

The Gunshot

We trudge through the wallowing mud
Guns explode dangerously overhead
We limp and stumble crying in pain
So near to death that we are halfway in Heaven itself
So nearly away from this hell zone
I pray for it to end
But it hasn't
And it won't
Suddenly
On nothing
Behind nothing
Opposite nothing
Between nothing
Under nothing
Above nothing
Before nothing
Through nothing
In death.

Hannah Pilley Rabbs (11)
St Paul's Catholic College, Burgess Hill

Shellshock

Shells, shells shocking soldiers
Rotten rats scurry through trenches

Blind warriors bleed and choke
Dangerously crossing no-man's-land

Shells, shells shocking soldiers
Rotten rats scurry through trenches

Soldiers stumble and sleep in trenches
Saying prayers as muddy boots
Trudge through muck and dirt.

Shells, shells shocking soldiers
Rotten rats scurry through trenches

Soldiers fight helplessly against enemies
Soldiers cry out in despair and hopelessness.

Darah Swinscoe (12)
St Paul's Catholic College, Burgess Hill

Far From Heaven, Closer To . . .

Through the wet dirty mud we walk hungrily
Towards the German army
Next to us it's deadly
Through us it's hurt
Outside us it's braveness
In us it's love
Near us it's torture
Far from us is family
But now it is *achievement!*

Isabelle Hecker (12)
St Paul's Catholic College, Burgess Hill

World War Scary

In the trenches we are scared and muddy
Opposite the opposition
Behind the thick mud
Before we get shot.

Between us in no-man's-land
Through the raging wind
Behind us is our lovely camp
Where I long to go back.

After I walked through the rotten bodies that still bleed
Their deaths left their friends wailing
The pain they must be in, I had to put them out of their misery
There seemed to be only one courageous soldier.

Suddenly, a lash of bullets shot me sorely all over
I try to move but just trudge
I choke and bleed and fall to my knees
It turns to darkness, I am praying prayers
With a *thud, thud, thud* and out cold I go.

Jack Parris (12)
St Paul's Catholic College, Burgess Hill

The Tell-Tale Heart

Round the corner it sounded zany
Round the corner was my friend Blake
I popped my head round to see what was happening
                                              to my friend Blake

Then I saw the shiny thing
It was a blade, I'm sure it was
And it was in Blake's hand
I was so sorry
I was shocked, I was scared
I'm next I was sure
Two weeks later in the wooden coffin
There was no cure.

Dave Tungate (13)
St Paul's Catholic College, Burgess Hill

The Tell-Tale Heart

The floorboards creaked and groaned under my weight
I crept along the lifeless corridor, walking to my doom
As I reached the end of the corridor I came upon a dark
                                        and desolate room
I approached the door, but in the way I found a crate
I pushed the crate and now as I look back I know I shouldn't have
Because beneath the crate . . .
Was a man but it wasn't the man that scared me most
It was the thing he held in his hand . . .
His heart, it had been torn out of him
And the hole it left was stuffed with sand
I turned to run, but found that the door had gone
And in its place was a grave and on the gravestone was . . .
My *name*
And before I knew it, I tripped, I stumbled and fell and fell
Until I hit the bottom of the bottomless pit
And then I felt the cold earth fall
And then I knew that I never should have come!

Alexander Bell (12)
St Paul's Catholic College, Burgess Hill

Hell On Earth

Wailing prayers, exploding death
Through mines and barbed wire
The fierce snowstorms freeze our toes
The deafening shells drive you mad
The rotten corpses attract rats like magnets
And lice crawl everywhere, even in your clothes.

The food is horrible, very little of it
Even in the night you do not find safety
And you're up and shooting at first light
Brave soldiers everywhere shedding tears and dying
Behind us our loving families
In front of us, Hell on Earth.

Emile Chasteauneuf (11)
St Paul's Catholic College, Burgess Hill

The Tell-Tale Heart

I creep into the darkness, sitting still
waiting for something to happen
I fall off my stool, shivering with fear
I feel a wind on my neck, a very unusual one
I bravely turn around to see two deadly bloodshot eyes
I let out a scream, only there was no sound
I float in the air knowing it was my last to live
Suddenly I drop in a dark and hard hole
I cut myself all over
When I turned around my heart stopped beating
When . . . I saw a rotting dead man with a hole in his chest
But the thing that frightened me most
Was he was holding his organs
When I heard a shovel and dirt fell on me
When I stopped breathing and that was the end of . . .

Georgina Clare Abbott (12)
St Paul's Catholic College, Burgess Hill

No-Man's-Land

Through the thick mud we duck and dive
Over and under the barbed wire
Live ammo whizzing above and worms and dead allies below
Opposite the enemy, behind the safety of the trenches
Rifles armed and guns blazing we start to run
As we fix on our bayonet, a bomb goes off
And there is smoke and dust in the air
As it clears I stand face to face with a German
I stood frozen when I felt a sharp pain in my chest
I look down and I find a knife has pierced my skin
I fall back and close my eyes
Death.

Rob Barnard-Voice (12)
St Paul's Catholic College, Burgess Hill

The Tell-Tale Heart

She gasped for breath as she thumped against the wall
Waiting for her doom to reveal all
With one last breath she went inside
To a place where she would never dare hide
A shadow appeared as the door creaked open
Her foot touched the floorboard which had been broken
She tried to scream but nothing came out
Help me, oh help me, is what she tried to shout
She fell and fell until she hit the bottom
What she fell in was all rough and rotten
The shadow which she had seen before
Was falling down towards the floor.

Lydia Berry (12)
St Paul's Catholic College, Burgess Hill

The Tell-Tale Heart

It follows me, I start to run
I feel its breath
Down my neck
It is dark, only one flickering lamp.

It chases me into the building
The floorboards creak and groan
As if they will break
Then I hear a colossal groan.

It had broken I was going to fall
But then I realise there's a sizeable hole
On the other side of the room
In the floor.

I ran to it
There was blood everywhere
I saw that he was blind
I heard a flapping of humungous wings.

Holly Watts (12)
St Paul's Catholic College, Burgess Hill

Black Death

A thundering sound of machine guns awoke me
The fierce brave soldiers bleed to death
As I am rotting in the trenches, helpless, in pain
Soldiers are wailing, praying and screaming to see light once more
As the Germans march with their thundering boots, Britain's trembling
All the soldiers can only see Black Death.

Thomas Rusbridge (11)
St Paul's Catholic College, Burgess Hill

The Tell-Tale Heart

One gloomy night
When the stars were shining bright
The person heard a creak
And the rain started to leak
In the house of Hell
Is it a man you cannot tell
I came closer and closer
The man got scared
As the murderer dared
To pull out a gun
Maybe just for fun
He pulled it back
Twas a vicious attack
Now the owner of the house of Hell
Can never tell
Whether the obnoxious beat
Is the cause of moving feet.

Connor Emery (12)
St Paul's Catholic College, Burgess Hill

The Tell-Tale Heart

There he lay beneath the rubble
He must have been in somewhat trouble
I went to help him but then I heard
The flapping wings of a colossal bird
I turned around and saw what I dread
I heard the sound and felt the lead
With all my strength from every muscle and bone
What I will do next was completely unknown
A figure emerged from behind the bird
He whispered something but what was that word?
My heart was pounding, I felt such fear
For here it came with my last tear
The word it said was tell-tale heart
For now it's my turn to depart
For now it's my turn to depar . . .

Alex Gorringe (13)
St Paul's Catholic College, Burgess Hill

The Misty Battle

The solders were choking on their blood
Those soldiers were in lots and lots of pain
The enemy were fierce and scary
The wounded fled to the trenches
But the enemy shot them before they could make it
It was muddy everywhere, blood was everywhere
Death was taking place everywhere.

Rory Bickley (11)
St Paul's Catholic College, Burgess Hill

The Tell-Tale Heart

There once lay a secret behind a door
A low tone beating under the floor
It contained a bursting urge to tell
With all its senses, touch and smell.

An object around the size of your fist
Kept its death story within the mist
Its body lay decomposing in mess
The whole mystery was one big guess.

I walked into the empty room
A shadow fell across the doom
I knew this would be my very last breath
For the creature that was looming was itself death.

Its eagle-like eyes stared coldly in mine
A roar, a scream, this was the time
It lingered over me, ready to eat
He ate my hands and then my feet.

He took off my chest and ripped out my heart
He had it down to a very fine art
He ripped the floorboards with all his might
He couldn't seem to get it right.

A tear ran down his pale white face
As he was putting the heart in place
The heart belonged to his old wife
As he had killed her with a knife.

Alexandra Pearson (13)
St Paul's Catholic College, Burgess Hill

War Stories

The fierce soldiers bravely limp to the trench
Muddy boots stumble to get back
Courageous men limp painfully
Fierce shells explode dangerously close.

Benjo Potts (12)
St Paul's Catholic College, Burgess Hill

The Thing

I run down the alleyway trembling with fright
Knowing this horror will last all the night
The monstrosity is near, I can smell his scent
He grumbled and growled, yet I know what he meant
His presence was nearer but somehow unreal
My stomach lurched and out came my meal
The monster had heard and roared with such power
I would die tonight and this was the hour
He raised his fist and killed with a blow
The end of my life, it was time to go
But it wouldn't stop there, after I was dead
It ripped off my limbs and pulled off my head
My corpse just lay there so battered and cold
I never even got the chance to grow old
I was wishing and hoping that this was a dream
But a passer-by let out a scream
This was definitely real, as real as can be
But would anyone care about dead old me?

Leah Riddell (12)
St Paul's Catholic College, Burgess Hill

The Tell-Tale Heart

Walking down the hallway careful as I go
Keeping to my own pace only as I know
Somewhere beneath my feet a body lays
And tonight it wakes just like the book says
Its heart stopped but soon it will beat
The king's throne it will take his seat.

The floor breaks in front of me, a hand stumbles through
The problem is kill it, I have no clue
I pick up an axe and swing it with all my strength
Cutting its head off at good length
The book was wrong, you can kill it
As the beast fell back down into its pit.

Adam Williams (13)
St Paul's Catholic College, Burgess Hill

My Beautiful Thing

In front of me lay the monster
As still as could be
He looked at me solemnly
I wonder what he sees
I see a beautiful wonderful creature
I made him
I gave him life, every brilliant feature.
The night is silent
Only him and me
And now I must leave you
My beautiful thing.

Cameron Fyall (12)
St Paul's Catholic College, Burgess Hill

Mystery And Suspense Poem

Once, twice, thrice
A smash at the door
What is it?
I don't know
Roaring, scratching, smashing the door
A moment
Cold, quiet
I'm scared
Huddled in a corner
A smash at the door
Breaks one corner
I close my eyes
I hear one more smash
I never wake up.

Nicholas Burns (13)
St Paul's Catholic College, Burgess Hill

The Tell-Tale Heart

The door screamed as it drifted open
I lightly paced along the dusty floorboards, a shiver went down

my spine

I crawled up the steps
I knew I should not have come, but I couldn't turn back
I caught a spider in my hand as I brushed past the silky webs
The room was full of ancient furniture
I leaned over the dusty table
A beam of misty light revealed a body
A body on the floor
I turned around in fright, ran for the door
The door was gone
I ran to the other side of the room
Searching
Searching for life
What's the point?

Tom Still (12)
St Paul's Catholic College, Burgess Hill

Trench Warfare

Soldiers stumble, boots bleed
Soldiers pray as deadly shells explode in the muddy ground
Enemies shoot the helpless soldiers
Laying in the rotten mud
Soldiers stumble bravely towards the enemy
Blind to the fact that death awaits them.

Alastair McGinness (11)
St Paul's Catholic College, Burgess Hill

The Tell-Tale Heart

As I walk I feel a shiver
My blood runs cold
The moon shines bright

I see a house
Old and dull
Shall I go in?

As I walk I hear a sound
Boom, boom!
It's getting louder

The house is far
Still I wonder
Why I go?

The grounds are full of graves
As I get closer I see a stone
But no name upon it

I enter the house
The door, large and wooden
The corridor in front of me never-ending

As I walk
I see a floorboard
One nail missing

A heart beating, under the floor
A hand appears
Grabs my ankle

There I lie
Stone-cold!

Alice Parton (12)
St Paul's Catholic College, Burgess Hill

The Tell-Tale Heart

Through the darkest night
There walked in the ugliest sight
He and his fear shuddered
He found a body murdered
This was his only chance
He made his way through the gas

He sensed the touch of a vampire
But he could feel the wind's lustre
With no time he fell to the ground
His heart stopped beating, he was bound
The birds stopped squawking
And the squirrels started peeking
Everything was still . . .

Ann-Mariya Mathews (13)
St Paul's Catholic College, Burgess Hill

The Tell-Tale Heart

The pernicious barbaric man
Killed the young fellow with a frying pan
And then the mangled body
Was bound in the lounge, the carpet was bloody
And then the corpse's wife
Came back with a knife
She caught the murderer not at his best
She got him in the corner and struck him in the chest
The killer forever deceased
The wife's anguish has ceased
Now the ghost haunts the house once every new moon
And the frying pan has become a spoon.

Michael Szweda (12)
St Paul's Catholic College, Burgess Hill

The Tell-Tale Heart

There was a man with piercing eyes
That found beneath the floorboard bed
A man that was dead!

One day a man partly blind was making himself tea
He walked into the kitchen to find a key
This key opened a door, but which
He found this door and inside the room was nothing, it was empty.

He walked straight in, a bird
He carried on and a creak he heard
The bird tapped on one of the floorboards
He opened it up and saw a sword

It was in a man
Blood dripping down his hand
And what he does not know
That it was I who put him there!

Bryony Rushton (12)
St Paul's Catholic College, Burgess Hill

The Tell-Tale Heart

In a frightful eerie room
Ghouls get ready to seal your doom
Running rapidly, no escape
The vampire opens his big black cape
The gormless eyes of the ancient paintings
My heart is pounding, my soul is fainting.

Olajide Buckley (12)
St Paul's Catholic College, Burgess Hill

Young Writers Information

We hope you have enjoyed reading this book - and that you will continue to enjoy it in the coming years.

If you like reading and writing poetry drop us a line, or give us a call, and we'll send you a free information pack.

Alternatively if you would like to order further copies of this book or any of our other titles, then please give us a call or log onto our website at www.youngwriters.co.uk

Young Writers Information
Remus House
Coltsfoot Drive
Peterborough
PE2 9JX

(01733) 890066